40 DAY PRAYER

COVENANT

FOLLOWING JESUS TOGETHER

GRACE	Dear Father, thank you for your grace that has made me one of your dearly loved children.
LOVE	By your grace make knowing, loving and obeying you my highest priority.
COMPASSION	Empower me to love others the way you love me.
REPENTANCE	Wash me clean from every sin.
WORSHIP	Enable me to praise you, O Lord, with all my heart.
COMMITMENT	Jesus, be Lord of my life today in new ways, and change me any way you want!
DEPENDENCE	Fill me with your Holy Spirit.
INFLUENCE	Make me an instrument of your grace, truth, forgiveness, righteousness and justice.
DISCIPLESHIP	Use me today for your glory, and to invite others to follow Jesus Christ as Lord.
AUTHORITY	I pray in the name of Jesus. Amen.

40 DAY PRAYER COVENANT

THE VISION

To see the Prayer Covenant be a catalyst for an awakening to Jesus Christ as Lord throughout the United States and the world.

THE MISSION

For the Prayer Covenant to be a catalyst to commit our lives to Jesus Christ as Lord daily with persons who will do the same with others.

INSTRUCTIONS

1 Consider praying this prayer for 10 days before sharing it with others.

2 Ask Jesus to forgive your sins, and help you stop your sin patterns.

3 Invite the Holy Spirit to guide and empower you to pray.

4 Select a quiet place and time to pray unhurriedly.

5 Find at least one prayer partner and hold each other accountable.

6 Ask God to show you others whom you might invite into this Prayer Covenant.

7 Ask your Heavenly Father for lifelong growth in prayer, wisdom, maturity, and love.

THE PRAYER COVENANT

COVENANT

FOLLOWING JESUS TOGETHER

JERRY R. KIRK

With Stephen D. Eyre

40 Day Prayer Covenant Inc.
800 Compton Road, Suite 9224
Cincinnati, OH 45231
www.theprayercovenant.org

Materials to supplement **The Prayer Covenant:** *Following Jesus Together* are available online at the website, **www.theprayercovenant.org** including a children's version and free multiple language versions of the 40 Day Payer Covenant Card. Copies of the books are available at special discounts for bulk purchases.

Design by Sound Press

ISBN 978-0-9899525-0-7

Library of Congress Control number: 2007012345

Printed in the United States of America

ENDORSEMENTS

It has been my joy to know and respect Jerry Kirk for nearly forty years. The Prayer Covenant is a personification of his heart, passion and life. I highly commend this book to you. It is a powerful and practical invitation from the heart of a faithful servant of our Lord Jesus Christ.

— **DR. PAUL CEDAR**, Chairman of Mission American Coalition, Palm Desert CA

Almost 90% of our congregation entered into the Prayer Covenant and it has shifted our culture. There is now an atmosphere of prayer; there is an attitude of warfare in prayer; and there is a mindset of keeping each other's spirit up in prayer. As the senior leader of our congregation, I attribute this cultural shift of prayer to The 40-Day Prayer Covenant. We are moving from a "house that prays" to a "house of prayer."

— **JERRY CULBRETH**, Senior Elder and Apostle, Tryed Stone New Beginning Church, Cincinnati, Ohio

The friendship of Dr. Jerry Kirk and his example of humble Christian leadership has been a great blessing in my life. In the 40 Day Prayer Covenant, Dr. Kirk shares with us the wisdom and insights that are the fruit of his own rich prayer life. Moreover, the 40 Day Prayer Covenant gives us an immensely practical tool to mutually challenge and support fellow disciples in surrendering our hearts more completely to Jesus.

— **MOST REVEREND JOSEPH F. NAUMANN**, D.D., Archbishop, Kansas City, Kansas

In September of 1971, Jerry and I entered into a Prayer Covenant. This practice of prayer led to the Lord calling me to College Hill Presbyterian Church to serve with Jerry and a divinely gifted staff for 18 years! I praise

the Lord for this life-changing experience and for all the serendipities that came through the Prayer Covenant.

— **DR. RON RAND**, Director, UpBuilding Ministries, Fort Myers, Florida

Jerry Kirk has been helpful to many in their spiritual journey. In The 40 Day Prayer Covenant: Following Jesus Together, he is helpful again to those who follow Jesus, or want to follow Him more closely. The covenant to pray reminds us that as Christians we live in community and need the support of each other to become the people God calls us to be. This book will enrich that journey, sharpen our spirits, and bring us closer to the Lord we love and serve. I commend its reading to you.

— **COMMISSIONER WILLIAM A. ROBERTS**, Chief of the Staff, The Salvation Army International Headquarters, London, England

Epidemiologists trying to understand a pandemic stand in front of giant video screens covered with dots connected by lines. The researchers want to trace back all the connections between persons carrying the disease. Similarly, Spirit-breathed movements spread through connections among believers—connections often founded on prayer. God has whispered to Jerry Kirk a marvelous plan for linking countless numbers of believers in prayer-filled relationships. Some of those relationships will last 40 days and some will last a lifetime—but all will be part of setting the sails for the coming Christ awakening.

— **DR. RICHARD ROSS**, Professor of Student Ministry, Southwestern Seminary, Fort Worth, Texas

Despite its mundane title this robust book is a spiritual feast. The Prayer Covenant takes us into new depths of spiritual life. It soars in its implications for revival and renewal, personally and corporately. The current buzz among Pastors focuses on Missional and Discipleship activities, but few books take us as deeply into the simple but profound aspects of discipleship. We are moved from personal devotions to personal action *and servant leadership. Thankfully we can read numerous examples from the lives of real people to inspire and motivate us to grow and change.*

— **DR. GARY R. SWEETEN**, Founder, Sweeten Life Systems, Inc., Cincinnati. Ohio

There are a few things that every parent desires to give a child. There are a very few things for which God "tells" us to pray. Jerry Kirk has assembled a prayer that is a combination of both of these. It is a prayer that God answers in detail. After praying it for years, I can say this prayer is the most life changing prayer that I have prayed or come across. It not only leads us into a greater intimacy with the Father, Jesus and the Holy Spirit, it also brings us into a closer covenant relationship with those for whom we pray. Thank you Jerry for your obedience, wisdom, humility and love and especially for the way that you share these with so many.

— **FORD TAYLOR**, Founder, The FSH Group/Transformational Leadership/Transformation Cincinnati N. Kentucky, Terrace Park, Ohio

The journey to maturity in Christ is marked by faith and practice, that is a long obedience in the same direction. Jerry Kirk shares his story of combining faith and practice for over six decades in committed use of the simple yet profound tool called the 40 Day Prayer Covenant. This book will bless you and invite you into a life of prayer from the heart that will bless others as well.

— **SIBYL TOWNER**, Co-founder and Spiritual Director for OneLifeMaps, Co-Director of The Springs, Retreat Center, Oldenburg, Indiana

I had the privilege of coming to know Jesus Christ at the funeral of my sister-in-law in October, 2010. I began to pray the Prayer Covenant the next day and I have been praying the Prayer Covenant ever since. I'm thrilled that you are reading this book.

— **TONY TRABERT**, World Tennis Champion, Member of the Hall of Fame, Chairman of the Tennis Hall of Fame (ret.), Ponte Vedra, Florida

Through Scripture, personal insights from his years of following Jesus, and candid glimpses into his own personal life Jerry Kirk reminds us of the transforming grace of God as it is experienced in prayer, particularly covenant prayer with others. In The Prayer Covenant he shows us the pathway and extends to us the invitation to an intimacy with God and others through these covenant times of prayer. My own life has been greatly enriched by these seasons of covenant prayer as I have linked my heart with friends before God. As I read this book and reflected on my walk with Christ I have been challenged to pursue God with greater passion and to do so in the company of others who share that same passion. It might just change your life!

— **DR. J. K. WARRICK**, General Superintendent of the Church of the Nazarene, Lenexa, KS

DEDICATION

To Patricia Snyder Kirk, my faithful and gracious wife for fifty-seven years. You are God's most special gift to me and our family; mother of five, grandmother of twenty-eight, and great grandmother of sixteen. You have lovingly and sacrificially nurtured each member of the family.

In addition, I give thanks to our two sons, Timothy and Stephen, who gave wise counsel in finalizing the Prayer Covenant, and to our three daughters, Kimberly Hahn, Kari Harrington, Kristen Holsclaw, and the five spouses for your commitment to the Lord and your families. You give me great hope for this and future generations. "Thank you for your faithfulness and for your precious children and grandchildren."

Finally, I thank Stephen Eyre, my co-author, for his unusual skill, diligence, sensitivity and partnership in the Lord. Without you this book would not have come to God's people in this way and at this time.

FOREWORD

You can know someone for decades, and still they surprise you!

I first met Jerry Kirk in 1975 at College Hill Presbyterian Church in Cincinnati where he was senior pastor. His reputation as a Jesus follower of vision, passion and compassion preceded him. I was not disappointed.

Subsequently, intersecting with Jerry in a variety of settings – from promoting world missions, to serving prayer movements, to encouraging racial reconciliation, to efforts at denominational renewal, to coalitions against pornographic trade, to fostering national spiritual revival – I've witnessed the heights of his vision, depths of his passion and breadth of his compassion increase in ways only a person filled with the life of Christ could expect.

But it was in 2008, working together on a facilitation team for a nationwide gathering of young people to celebrate the supremacy of Jesus, when Jerry really surprised me. That's when I saw the true extent of his convictions about prayer. For him, boundless potential lies in concerted, covenanted, consistent intercession focused on re-awakening Christians to the lordship of Jesus.

That's the promise of this book.

The Prayer Covenant distills decades of Jerry's prayerful ministry into one, profoundly simple, but wholly unique, strategy: Commit to join one other believer, for forty days, in a ten-fold prayer, focused on (what I call) a "Christ Awakening", for each other (and others). In over 30 years working to accelerate united prayer throughout the global church I've never seen any approach like this, so full of possibilities yet so practical anyone can do it.

But watch out – remember, I warned you this man is full of surprises!

The fact is, the book is really not about getting us to pray as it is about getting us to Christ.

Listen to Jerry in his own words (from throughout the book):

- "The Lordship of Christ is the heart of the Prayer Covenant."

- "This Covenant is my attempt to capture the essence of Christian discipleship, the essence of following Christ as Lord."

- "It is the vision of exalting Christ through praying and spreading the Prayer Covenant that led to writing this book."

- "My goal is not really to get people to pray the Prayer Covenant. The goal is to 'follow Jesus together' for the rest of our lives."

And finally, my favorite quote:

- "I work on (the Covenant) all the time, because I am asking God for an awakening to Jesus Christ as Lord throughout the U.S. and the world."

You'll find this little volume to be user-friendly, easy to follow, fascinating, relational, vulnerable, pragmatic, inspiring – and so full of hope. Just like the author himself!

And Jerry throws in some great stories, to boot!

The Prayer Covenant plows new ground for seeking the Christ Awakening for which multitudes are yearning. It is for any two Christians ready to "follow Jesus together" in a great adventure: united, reciprocal prayer for the fame and reign of God's Son.

Don't miss out on it!

DAVID BRYANT, President, Proclaim Hope, Author, Christ Is All!

TABLE OF CONTENTS

FOLLOWING JESUS TOGETHER

IN 1967, A LEADING BUSINESSMAN in Pittsburgh challenged me to join him in a Prayer Covenant that profoundly changed my life and ministry. He reminded me of the words of Jesus in Luke 9:23: "If anyone would come after me, he must deny himself and take up his cross daily and follow me." Jesus makes it clear: to follow him, we are called to die to self daily. Then this businessman referred to 2 Chronicles 15:12, which says, "They entered into a covenant to seek the Lord, the God of their ancestors, with all their heart and soul."

He asked me, "Jerry, do you want to follow Jesus that way? Do you want him to be Lord of your life, and are you willing to ask him to be Lord at the beginning of every day for thirty days? If you do, will you then ask him to be Lord of my life for that day? If you do, I will pray the same prayer at the beginning of every day for my life and then for your life. Are you willing to join me in this covenant to follow Jesus together flat out and to hold each other accountable to fulfill our commitment?"

My response was immediate and enthusiastic: "Yes! Yes! And yes! I would love to pray that prayer each day for thirty days and then pray it over you. And I am ready to be held accountable to that covenant by you. I want Jesus to be Lord of my life." That day, he and I sealed our commitment to Christ and each other on our knees in a dorm room at Wilson College in eastern Pennsylvania, the site of the conference we were attending.

I will tell you more about what led to this experience later in this book. What I want you to know right now is that this simple but challenging prayer and partnership brought new vigor and vitality to my relationship with Christ and the people closest to me, including my family, friends, and congregation. I learned then, and by our friendship through the years, that following Jesus together increased my confidence in the grace and love of God, the power of prayer, and my expectation that God would use me for his glory. This prayer unleashed me to follow Jesus with new zest and strength and to believe that God would use me on a regular basis to bring people to know Christ and follow him passionately.

Are you ready for the joy and adventure that only comes from a growing commitment to Jesus Christ as Lord? Do you desire that God use you in the lives of others on a daily basis? If so, then this book and the Prayer Covenant it expounds are for you in your journey of Christian discipleship.

Since 1967, I have joined in thousands of Prayer Covenants that have strengthened me greatly. The Prayer Covenant is a life-changing prayer that can last a lifetime. It binds people's lives together under the lordship of Jesus Christ and inspires deeper levels of obedience and discipleship. I have come back to it again and again with new vigor and strength. These years of ministry have been an incredible grace gift from God. While this prayer has grown in length, the essence is always the same—"Jesus, be Lord of my life"—and it continues to guide and form me on a daily basis.

TOGETHER

The lordship of Christ is the heart of the Prayer Covenant. The spirit and soul of the Prayer Covenant is that we live under the lordship of Christ together with fellow believers. It is a great joy to follow Jesus; it is the greatest joy to follow Jesus with others. The first disciples were called to be with Jesus, certainly, but by Jesus' call they were placed into a shared relationship with him and each other. That's the point of Jesus' new command: "A new command I give you: Love one another. As I have loved you, so you must love one another" (John 13:34).

Once we have the eyes to see it, this relational dynamic is central to the entire Bible and runs throughout the Old Testament to the New. God isn't just calling out individuals; he is calling out a *people* to follow him together. When he delivers Israel from slavery in Egypt he said, "Although the whole earth is mine, you will be for me a kingdom of priests and a holy nation" (Exodus 19:5-6).

Our modern world is so self-centered and individualistic that we miss the relational theme running through the Bible. Think how Jesus teaches us to pray. What are the very first words in his prayer? They are "Our Father." For most of us, we may say, "Our Father," but we think "My Father." The first pagans who were converted to Christ in the classical world were self-centered too. That is why Peter writes to these new believers: "But you are a chosen people, a royal priesthood, a holy nation, a people belonging to God, that you may declare the praises of him who called you out of darkness into his wonderful light. Once you were not a people, but now you are the people of God; once you had not received mercy, but now you have received mercy" (1 Peter 2:9-10). Peter wants us to understand that God has brought us together, and it is together that we bring him glory.

The joy of following Jesus together was an integral part of the ministry at College Hill Presbyterian Church in Cincinnati, where the Prayer Covenant grew from one simple phrase to the ten lines you will read about in this book. I arrived as pastor in November 1967. If I often felt inadequate and over my head in ministering to

650 Presbyterians in my prior congregation, you can imagine how I felt when called to lead a congregation of 2,300 in Cincinnati.

The Sunday before arriving in Cincinnati, seventeen people joined me in the Prayer Covenant. This meant seventeen people were praying daily for me that Jesus would be Lord of my life as I began my ministry at College Hill. My first Friday night there, the middle-aged couples group was meeting at the church to share a meal and hear the personal story of Bob Sheck, an executive with Procter & Gamble. At forty-five, he was leaving the business world, going to seminary, and becoming a pastor. As the new pastor, I was asked to give a five-minute closing response following his message.

It was an amazing evening with wonderful food, lots of fun, and a warm and wholesome fellowship. Bob's witness of coming to Christ, his influence among his business associates, and his sense of call to ministry were contagious. The whole time I was listening to him, I was talking to God inwardly: "Lord, surely you don't want me to do something crazy. Give me your wisdom. Guide me in what to say. This is my first meeting as their pastor, and their first exposure to me apart from the pulpit. I'm thirty-five years old and look like twenty-five. Lord, this is a sophisticated congregation. Help me get acquainted gradually and have the opportunity to get to know them as persons and learn their names, etc., etc., etc. Please use me."

Bob finished and it was time for the new pastor to speak. I told them how pleased I was to be part of their fellowship for this special evening and how I had come to know the Lord and experience Christ in ways similar to Bob. I told them how much I respected him for his sacrificial decision to leave the business world at forty-five and to pay for three years of graduate education at seminary while supporting his family, knowing all the time that at the end he would receive a salary approximately half of what he was making at Procter & Gamble.

Then I decided to have a Presbyterian altar call. Do you know what that is? It is subtle. It is low-key. This is what I said: "I can tell that we have been blessed tonight. God has met us in this place. Some of us might want to stay around and talk about it. If that is true for you, come back into the parlor fifteen minutes after we break, and we will discuss our response to what we have heard."

Seventeen people came into the parlor. We put the chairs into a circle, and I turned to the person on my left. "Lois, what led you to come into the parlor, and what are your thoughts about what we have heard from Bob? Let's go around the circle with each one of you sharing your thoughts. When we are done, we will end our evening."

When we finished going around the circle, I asked if they would like me to share what I believed God might be doing among us. Everyone responded affirmatively. I told them about the Prayer Covenant and how it had profoundly changed my life and ministry.

I said to them, "Would any of you like to join me in praying for each other daily, giving as much of ourselves as we can to as much of Christ as we understand, and asking Jesus to be the Lord of our lives each day?" Their response was spontaneous and overwhelming. "Yes! We want to join you in that prayer," they said, and they did. I now had thirty-four people for whom I was praying and who were praying daily for me that Jesus would be Lord of my life and guide me to be God's pastor for the College Hill Presbyterian congregation. Can you imagine the encouragement and strength these people and their prayers gave me?

The Prayer Covenant became a trigger that inspired conversations about the Lord rather than just the recent Cincinnati Reds baseball game or the Bengals football game. College Hill was an exciting place to grow spiritually, and it became an equipping center for our own people and for thousands of pastors and lay leaders from across the country and around the world. The Prayer Covenant inspired us to follow Jesus Christ as Lord during my first year at College Hill, and over seven hundred people either came to Christ for the first time or recommitted their lives to him during those months. I felt like I was riding a whale through the ocean. God was changing us all. This was the beginning of a twenty-year pastorate that continually changed my life and ministry, and strengthened our marriage and family of five children.

LEADING TOGETHER

As the ministry of the Lord grew at College Hill, we had visits from leaders from around the country. We were frequently asked, "What's the key to this place? It's alive!" The answer to that question was that God assembled a staff of gifted people who were highly motivated and deeply committed to the lordship of Christ. We just kept growing deeper in following Jesus together, and that overflowed in tremendous spiritual blessings.

Gary Sweeten, Ron Rand, Sibyl and Dick Towner, Harry Causey, Alice Peterson, and Bob Hauck were among the many staff that kept equipping people to grow in Christ. In fact, they were a team gifted far beyond me. My role was helping them work together while keeping the focus on the lordship of Christ. The team worked so well together that I only led one staff meeting in my last ten years. Dick, who led the meetings, had the gift of administration. I asked Gary, who was gifted in relational dynamics, to be the team facilitator, helping us grow together as a highly functional and godly team. Ron Rand later became co-pastor. Sarah Blanken Kahmann, my Ministry Assistant, multiplied my effectiveness within the congregation and far beyond by her administrative and pastoral skills.

There are several different ways that teams can work together. A baseball team is composed of individuals who fill their positions as a catcher, pitcher, first baseman, etc., and who seem almost to work by themselves. Then there is a football team, in which the quarterback calls the shots and everyone has their prescribed and preplanned role in the play. Then there is a basketball team, which works together passing the ball back and forth, keying off one another as each takes turns making decisions and taking shots. Although a basketball team does have a leader in its point guard, the decision making is more evenly distributed than in baseball or football. We were more like a basketball team. Everyone kept the ball moving in order to travel down the court and reach the goal of proclaiming Christ and glorifying God.

Our commitment to one another to work together affected everything, even our decisions to consider calls to new ministry positions at other churches or Christian ministries. Gary was asked to be the dean of students at Gordon-Conwell Theological Seminary. He brought the decision to the team of staff and elders. After prayer and discussion, the team felt that God was not calling him away to the seminary but to move into a new position of Christian discipleship at College Hill. Gary submitted to the voice of the Lord through the shared leadership and elders, and God blessed his obedience and humility. He went on to develop courses such as Apples of Gold and Rational Christian Thinking that have been used by hundreds of churches around the world.

As the team developed, I moved from preaching regularly to three times a month, and then finally to preaching only twice a month. The staff were so gifted and moved in such power that I felt it was important for them to share the pulpit with me. Fellow pastors at other churches were amazed and shocked when I told them about my preaching schedule—saying their congregations would not allow them to do such a thing. The congregation at College Hill loved the variety and gifting of the staff and didn't have a problem with it, because the staff was so strong and had so much wisdom to give. This shared preaching schedule allowed the gifts of the others to come front and center and we all knew they were helping lead the entire congregation.

The result of this shared preaching was that I was freed to be more in touch with people pastorally. More than that, my preaching was life changing because I wasn't preaching all the time. My gift was exhortation, and I could do that both from the pulpit and sitting in a counseling session. And even beyond that, the shared preaching schedule gave me time to lead preaching missions at other churches and even to be an adjunct professor at Fuller Theological Seminary in Pasadena. Whether I was at College Hill or somewhere else, the church continued to grow and develop as the staff team worked together in ministry. But it was more than just the staff; around each of the staff, ministry teams grew and developed as well. Gifts and ministry were unleashed as members of the church discovered the power and joy of following Jesus together in evangelism, discipleship, children's ministry, youth ministry, worship, and music.

THE JOY OF FOLLOWING JESUS TOGETHER

You may or may not be on a staff team, but you can know the joy of being in relationships that bring the joy of following Jesus together. One pastor I know discovered the joy of following Jesus together with fellow students in college: five students "just happened" to run into one another after church one evening. They attended different colleges and didn't know each other well, so they went out together for coffee just to become acquainted. Then they went over to one student's apartment for prayer and Bible study. They didn't really know how to study the Bible, nor were they experienced in prayer. However, as they talked and even argued about such subjects as the Bible and evolution, and as they spent time in prayer, something special began to happen. God was present and the Spirit moved. After the meeting broke up, one person said, "There is such joy being here with God and with you all. Let's do this next week." From that first meeting they began to meet weekly, and spiritual energy flowed out to touch their church, including people of all ages, and to impact their campuses for Christ.

What those students shared was more than just Christian fellowship; it was fellowship with a purpose. They were hungry to follow Jesus together. It transformed their lives and lots of other lives as well. That's what the Prayer Covenant is about. It provides a tool, a means by which we can be connected with God and each other.

The Prayer Covenant is my attempt to capture in prayer the essence of Christian discipleship, the essence of following Christ as Lord, the essence of what it means to do whatever we do "for the glory of God." It is a living document that seeks to aid us in living lives that are God-centered, Christ-exalting, Holy Spirit-led and empowered. We live these lives for God and others, and in fellowship with God and others. Dietrich Bonhoeffer referred to Christ as the "man for others." The person who follows Jesus will be a person whose life is lived for God and for others—seeking them, serving them, lifting them up, and in turn receiving these same precious gifts from them. I've learned that God's grace flows in many directions. When two or more people truly engage with one another around the person of Jesus, grace, mercy, and love flow between God and God's people. I have also learned that wanting to share together in fellowship and ministry is essential, but it is not enough. We need channels, mechanisms and means to do so—that is why we have prayer meetings, committee meetings, and even fellowship dinners. I have found the Prayer Covenant to be a powerful mechanism that provides the means for us to share and participate in the grace of God.

THE PRAYER COVENANT IS A TOOL

Why do we need a written prayer in order to share a Prayer Covenant? Can't we just agree to pray for each other? Isn't it better just to pray whatever comes to mind? Of course you can pray informally. God blesses both approaches. But the tradition of using a written prayer goes all the way back to our Lord Jesus Christ and the prayer he gave us to pray. And there are many throughout the two thousand years of Christian history who have found great help from written prayers. We have many mature brothers and sisters from ages past who have attained levels of spiritual maturity that you and I may never attain—but their prayers can take us beyond ourselves. Praying what comes to mind does not always result in a well-rounded prayer, as we are in stages of maturity. What we pray as a ten-year-old is not what we will pray when we are twenty or when we are forty.

I want to be clear here. The Prayer Covenant is not the only prayer you can pray or should pray. I offer it as a tool that God has blessed in my life and the lives of many others. The Prayer Covenant has grown over the years from one simple phrase to a prayer with ten separate lines. This Prayer Covenant allows me to pray with fellow believers in essential areas of Christian life and ministry. In the Prayer Covenant we pray for:

1. **Grace**

2. **Love**

3. **Compassion**

4. **Repentance**

5. **Worship**

6. **Commitment**

7. **Dependence**

8. **Influence**

9. **Discipleship**

10. **Authority**

These are essential threads we read about in the Bible, threads that God is using to weave the tapestry of his will in his world. When we pray the Prayer Covenant, we are inviting God to work in and through us. We are joining him in his saving work in the world through Jesus Christ. When we pray the Prayer Covenant, good things happen. The benefits of the Prayer Covenant include:

1. **Opening up to grace and new life with God**

2. **Receiving grace to love God above all**

3. **Empowering us to love others**

4. **Reminding us of our need for repentance and forgiveness**

5. **Inspiring worship and praise**

6. **Focus on the lordship of Christ**

7. **Dependence on the Holy Spirit and his life in us**

8. **A balanced relationship between grace and truth**

9. **Living for God's glory and inviting others to follow Jesus Christ as Lord**

10. **Authority from Jesus and his powerful promises in prayer**

The key to praying this Prayer Covenant is praying it from the heart. One Presbyterian pastor I know grew up in another Christian tradition that used written prayers. Until he was a teenager he found the written prayers used in worship to be boring. Then one day it dawned on him that he was supposed to "mean what he prayed." That changed everything. When we pray we can just say the words; we can go through the motions with any prayer, including the Lord's Prayer. But something wonderful happens when we make a commitment to Christ Jesus from the heart and then faithfully, with passion, gusto and faith, pray this prayer. We will continue to be changed—transformed!

I have found that this prayer opens our lives to the life God intends and provides through Jesus and his Spirit living in us. Jesus is the one who said, "I have come that they [the sheep] may have life, and have it to the full" (John 10:10). He is the one who said, "I am the good shepherd. The good shepherd lays down his life for the sheep" (John 10:14). Again he said, "I am the vine; you are the branches. If you remain in me and I in you, you will bear much fruit; apart from me you can do nothing" (John 15:5). In that passage, shortly before his death, Jesus calls us to love the way he loves and to obey him and the Father the way he obeys the Father. God's plan is that the Christian life is to be a joy-filled life and adventure, including bearing much fruit.

The strongest motivation for praying the Prayer Covenant is that God answers prayer in accordance with his will. When we pray for ourselves and for each other "that Jesus be Lord of our lives," we know that is the will of God because he says so. Therefore, we know God will answer that prayer. As you read this book you will explore the scriptural foundations for answered prayer. Faith will grow; expectancy will grow; confidence and power in prayer will grow; impact on the lives of those around you will grow, often exponentially.

THE 40 DAY PRAYER COVENANT

Throughout the years, I have used the Prayer Covenant in a set time frame. For instance, you will find a 40 Day Prayer Covenant Card included in this book. You can also log on to **www.theprayercovenant.org** and download a copy of The 40 Day Prayer Covenant Card. Initially I invited people into a 30 Day Prayer Covenant because that was true to my original commitment, and because of the ease with which one can remember it—thirty days to a month. I liked a 30 Day Prayer Covenant because it helped to have a limited time frame. It's too overwhelming for most of us to make a prayer covenant that seems to have no end.

However, I recently changed from thirty days to forty days because of the special role forty has in biblical revelation. It rained forty days and forty nights when God judged the world in Noah's time

(Genesis 7:12). When God was providing Moses with the Ten Commandments on Mount Sinai, Moses fasted for forty days and forty nights (Exodus 24:18). After the episode of the golden calf, Moses spent another forty days before God (Exodus 34:28). In the new covenant, the New Testament, the Spirit led Jesus into the wilderness where he fasted and prayed for forty days (Matthew 4:1-2). So forty days is an important biblical number. There is no similar revelation in Scripture about the significance of the number thirty.

While I have entered into thousands of prayer covenants that end after thirty or forty days, there are some prayer partners that I find I am called to pray for far beyond any set time limit. Many others who have entered into the Prayer Covenant have discovered that they too feel called to keep on praying for their Prayer Covenant partners beyond any time limit. Praying the Prayer Covenant may become a way of life for you. Sometimes you may have several prayer partners, and sometimes, just one or two. As you listen to the Lord for guidance about whom you pray for and how long you pray, you too will discover God guiding you.

It is always wise to start with limited and simple steps. So I am inviting you into a 40 Day Prayer Covenant and I encourage you to use the 40 Day Prayer Covenant Card. In this 40 Day Prayer Covenant, we are choosing to "follow Jesus together." This book is written to empower you to grow in prayer and to grow in prayer with fellow brothers and sisters in Christ. You may not feel comfortable right now in inviting someone to pray with you. That's ok. As you read through the following chapters, step-by-step, you will discover insights that will be helpful in praying and in joining with others in prayer.

You are deciding to take a significant step forward spiritually by asking Jesus to be Lord at the beginning of each day and then praying for another person. What will happen will be life changing for you and your covenant partner. But far more than that, God may well be using your prayers to change the eternal destinies of many in this nation and around the world.

REFLECTION QUESTIONS

Chapter 1   Following Jesus Together

1. The Prayer Covenant was a doorway to a new spiritual adventure and turning point in my life. What comes to mind when you hear the phrase "spiritual adventure"?

2. I was enthusiastic about the invitation to surrender to the Lordship of Jesus Christ. How do you feel about such an invitation? What concerns do you have?

3. One of the essential dynamics of the Prayer Covenant is that we share it with others. Why is this beneficial?

4. Not everyone feels comfortable using a written prayer—that is, a prayer that is not spontaneous but composed. What concerns do you have about using a written prayer? What benefits can you think of?

5. I list ten benefits of the prayer covenant that we will explore in coming chapters. Which of these are you especially interested in exploring?

CHAPTER 2
GRACE

THE FIRST LINE OF THE Prayer Covenant is, "Dear Father, thank you for your grace that has made me one of your dearly loved children." Grace and love go hand-in-hand, as God does not love us because we deserve it but because he is gracious.

Hearing about God's grace and love is a stumbling block for many people, because these words don't match their experience. They hear that God loves them, but they don't believe those words are true for their lives—they don't feel that they are, indeed, one of God's dearly loved children. They don't feel they measure up. Both from my personal experience and in ministry to others, I have come to the conclusion that we all have damaged receiving mechanisms when it comes to receiving fully the love and grace of God.

One afternoon in southern California, I was to be interviewed on TV for the first time. I had founded pureHOPE while serving as pastor of College Hill. (If you do not know of it, I hope you will take time to learn about pureHOPE at http://purehope.net.) The vision of pureHOPE is a world free of sexual exploitation and brokenness, and it has a mission of providing Christian solutions in a sexualized culture, equipping individuals, families, and churches to pursue sexual purity and oppose sexual exploitation. I took a one-year leave of absence from pastoring the church in order to give myself full time to help protect children and families from sexual exploitation, molestation, and pornography.

I had never been on TV so arrived early in hopes of overcoming my nervousness. The person who was to interview me had not yet arrived, and the program was to start in fifteen minutes. This did not help quiet my nerves. When she finally walked through the door, I was surprised. For some reason, I had not been expecting the interviewer to be a woman. She was a woman, and she was gorgeous. I had no idea until later that she had been Miss California. To be honest, I lost my concentration on our subject of sexual exploitation and pornography momentarily. But we proceeded with the interview, and I was told it went well. She was pleased with the result, and I was pleased that it was over.

After the interview she invited me and our vice president, Deen Kaplan, to have lunch with her and her husband. Early in the conversation she shocked me a second time. "Dr. Kirk," she said, "I have never known if anyone loves me."

How was it possible that this beautiful woman could say such a thing? I couldn't believe what I heard. I looked at her across the table and asked, "What did you say?"

"I said, I have never known whether anyone loved me." She explained, "My father never told me he loved me. As far as I know, he never held me. My husband tells me he loves me, but I don't know whether he loves me or only loves my body. My friends tell me they love me, but I don't know whether they love me or merely enjoy being seen with me. I have never known whether anyone really loves me." This was not the first time her husband heard these words. He was grateful that we could talk about her concern.

We spent the next hour talking about the love of God revealed in Jesus Christ and how she could know that love for herself and for her marriage. I wanted her to understand and believe that her receiving mechanism, which had been so damaged by her father and others, could be healed and restored.

I will never forget that lunch. God used our discussion to sensitize me in new ways. I became more aware that I also have a damaged receiving mechanism—and that all of us do. Maybe it's because of harsh words from a parent or sibling, from a teacher or coach, friend or teammate. Maybe it's from broken relationships that have never been healed, or from experiences of rejection and betrayal. Maybe it's from not being accepted by peers, or from personal, spiritual, or moral failure. Our damaged receiving mechanism often comes from bad choices or bad experiences with some of God's people not measuring up to expectations. These and many other things damage our receiving mechanism and our capacity to receive God's love and the love of others. We find it hard to believe we are of value—that we are special—that we are loved. No doubt Peter and Paul did not feel worthy of Jesus' love either. The good news is that God's gracious love finds a way to get through, and so we pray, "Dear Father, thank you for your grace that has made me one of your dearly loved children."

GRACE

The apostle Paul had so deeply experienced God's grace that he was transformed, and that grace inspired many of his letters in the New Testament. Grace permeates his words because he personally knew the grace of God. Initially hostile to Christianity, using imprisonment and death as weapons, he sought to persecute and destroy the followers of Jesus Christ. On his way to search for Christians in Damascus in order to apprehend them and bring them to Jerusalem, the risen and ascended Jesus confronted him on the road, knocking him off his horse: "Saul, Saul, why do you persecute me?"

"Who are you, Lord?" Saul asked.

"I am Jesus, whom you are persecuting," he replied. "Now get up and go into the city, and you will be told what you must do" (Acts 9:4-6).

Then, upon experiencing a blinding light, Saul had to be led into the city and could not see for three days. After his sight was restored, Saul the persecutor became Paul the apostle of grace to the Gentiles. Delivered from ignorance and murderous anger, he knew what it was to receive God's grace. At the end of his earthly life, in one of his last letters, he writes,

Even though I was once a blasphemer and a persecutor and a violent man, I was shown mercy because I acted in ignorance and unbelief. The grace of our Lord was poured out on me abundantly, along with the faith and love that are in Christ Jesus.

> Here is a trustworthy saying that deserves full acceptance: Christ Jesus came into the world to save sinners—of whom I am the worst. But for that very reason I was shown mercy so that in me, the worst of sinners, Christ Jesus might display his immense patience as an example for those who would believe on him and receive eternal life. (1 Timothy 1:13-16)

> This witness gives every one of us hope that "cannot be shaken" (Hebrews 12:28).

Like Paul, Peter experienced the grace of God again and again. One story of God's grace to Peter that has always touched me is the account of Peter's denial of Jesus on the night before the crucifixion, followed by the forgiveness that Jesus extends to him after his resurrection. Brash and confident during the entire three years of following Jesus, Peter was sure that even though all the other apostles might deny Jesus, he never would. I can almost hear him boasting, "You can count on me, Jesus. Even if all others fall away, I never will." Jesus, of course, knew better: "I tell you the truth, today—yes, tonight—before the rooster crows twice, you will disown me three times" (Mark 14:30).

Then we read the account of Peter's threefold denial a few hours later. Each denial becomes more emphatic, and the final time is the worst: "He began to call down curses on himself, and he swore to them, 'I don't know this man you're talking about'" (Mark 14:71). After that third denial, Jesus "turned and looked straight at Peter." Peter, of course, is cut to the heart. We read, "And he went outside and wept bitterly" (Luke 22:62).

If that were the end of the story, Peter would not have known or shared God's grace. But that was not the end of the story. Jesus appeared to Peter and the other apostles a number of times after his resurrection. One of those times was by the Sea of Galilee, when some of the apostles had gone fishing all night but caught nothing. As in an earlier experience (Luke 5:1-11), Jesus encouraged them to drop their nets on the opposite side of the boat. And, just as before, they caught a large number of fish and brought the nets to shore for a feast (John 21:1-8).

However, Jesus had bigger fish to fry. He wanted to reestablish his relationship with Peter by grace and restore Peter to his place of leadership among the apostles. He did so in a simple way by asking Peter three times, "Do you love me?" And after each affirmative response from Peter, Jesus commissions him: "Feed my lambs… Take care of my sheep… Feed my sheep" (John 21:15-17).

So often the most dedicated Christians are the most crushed by their sins. They lose their joy, freedom, and the power of the Lord. My appreciation of the depth of grace expressed by Jesus is strengthened when I remember that Jesus had made it very clear that public denial of him was a serious sin. "If any of you are ashamed of me and my words in this adulterous generation, the Son of Man will be ashamed of you when he comes in his Father's glory with the holy angels" (Mark 8:38). Peter was certainly ashamed of Jesus that night in the courtyard. And yet in the account by the Sea of Galilee, Jesus received Peter and restored him to leadership. That is grace! This is the way of God's grace to each of us.

As the first line of the Prayer Covenant expresses it, "Thank you for your grace that has made me one of your dearly loved children." Grace is the source of prayer and provides our invitation to pray. I have been greatly helped and encouraged by the words of Richard Foster. He writes, "We do not have to be bright or pure or filled with faith, or anything. That is what grace means, and not only are we saved by grace, we live by it as well. And we pray by it."[1]

C. S. Lewis was once walking through a study lounge at Oxford when he was stopped by a group of students who were discussing world religions. They asked him what was unique in Christianity from all the other religions. He paused thoughtfully for a moment, said one word, and then continued on his way. What was that word? "Grace."

GRACE AND HEALING

Even though I was given a wonderful family and a good start in life, I still find that damaged receiving mechanism in me, and so I have come to the conclusion that no matter who we are or what

---

1 (Richard Foster, *Prayer: Finding the Heart's True Home* [San Francisco: HarperSanFrancisco, 1992], p. 8).

our background, it takes God's grace to get his love through to us. I had good parents and an older brother who was an outstanding athlete. My father was a Rose Bowl football player, a coach of football, basketball, baseball, and track, a high school teacher, a lieutenant commander in the U.S. Navy, a state legislator, and later King County deputy treasurer of Seattle. He was a strong disciplinarian (like many coaches) who taught me obedience and thereby prepared me to follow Jesus as Lord obediently.

My mom was homecoming queen of Everett, Washington and later served six terms in the House of Representatives of the state of Washington, after my father left the House of Representatives in order to serve as deputy treasurer. She brought dynamism to our family. Dad was the disciplinarian. Mom was the source of nurture.

They loved me and were great providers and examples of integrity, but they did not know the Lord or his grace until years after I came to know Christ. Even then, my father found it difficult to understand and receive the grace and love of God in Christ. We were a performance-oriented family and I never felt that I lived up to their expectations.

I matured late. All through high school I was short in stature on the basketball court and felt "short of stature" with the more popular girls. I certainly felt inadequate in certain social situations. My confidence was greatly determined by other kids' response to me. I didn't know at that time that almost all teenagers struggle with feelings of inadequacy related to popularity, looks, and accomplishments in and out of the classroom. Those feelings of inadequacy within me would come back from time to time in my professional life as a youth leader and pastor.

In the mid-1960s, I was pastor at the New Wilmington Presbyterian Church across the street from Westminster (Presbyterian) College. We had nearly two hundred college kids worshiping with us each Sunday my last year there, as well as nearly thirty retired pastors and missionaries in the congregation. In addition, the president of the college, the vice president, all the deans, and over half of the faculty were in my congregation. I realized that if I were more highly trained, more gifted, and more effective, it would help me impact one of the leading liberal arts colleges for years to come. This realization not only challenged me, it made me feel inadequate!

At that time, there were two special women in my congregation with needs for healing and prayer: one dying from anxiety, the other shattered with fear. The first woman was down to 85 pounds—her doctor had given up on her. The other woman was expecting a second child, and her first delivery had almost killed her. She was filled with fear.

I took two congregational leaders, Bob Galbreath and Joy Tobin, to visit and pray with me for these women. After our prayer visits we returned to my study for a time of debriefing. We discovered that we too had our own needs for prayer: Bob was battling depression, and Joy was struggling with symptoms of multiple sclerosis—a tingling throughout her body like being plugged into a light socket. We prayed, and God answered.

They were surprised by my request for prayer—"feelings of inadequacy." I told them that my attention had become focused on myself. I was losing the joy and freedom of the Lord in my preaching. I knew those feelings of inadequacy were connected to my teenage experiences, and I knew I needed God's healing. Faithful to James 5, they laid hands on me, anointing me with oil, and prayed. Two things happened. First, I was healed of my feelings of inadequacy. My attention got off myself and back onto the Lord.

The second thing that happened was a new freedom and expectancy. I believed I was set free to minister within the whole body of Christ. This proved to be prophetic because of the surprising ways that I was given an expansive field of ministry beyond my hopes or expectations. When I served as chairman of the Greater Cincinnati Billy Graham Crusade, I was involved with over twenty denominations. During my twenty-year pastorate at College Hill, it became an equipping center, training pastors and leaders from over thirty denominations. This training was done primarily through Dr. Gary Sweeten, Dr. Ron Rand, and Mrs. Sibyl Towner. By God's grace I then became founder and president of pureHOPE and co-chairman of the *Religious Alliance Against Pornography*, which have served well over fifty denominations. That was a powerful prayer time!

I want to make a point here. In response to prayer, God graciously healed me from feelings of inadequacy. But he did not heal me of my inadequacy! My experience tells me that inadequacy is not usually the problem. We are all inadequate in some areas. It is feelings of inadequacy that crush our spirit and cause us such difficulty.

My healing of feelings of inadequacy was just one result of our prayers. Joy Tobin was at my door the next morning at eight o'clock. "It's gone! It's gone!"

"What's gone?" I asked.

"The tingling is gone! The Lord has healed me!"

I checked in with her a few years later, and again nearly forty years later, and it never came back. Bob Galbreath was healed of his depression, too, but the healing was neither total nor permanent. The need for healing from depression would come back from time to time and we would pray over him again; each time he found significant healing but never total relief.

The woman slowly dying from anxiety switched doctors the next week; the doctor changed her medication and the last I knew, she was a healthy 135 pounds and worshiping the Lord regularly. The woman who was overcome with fear found considerable, but not total, relief. A few days before the baby was due, her doctor decided to perform a C-section right away and not wait for the due date. Good thing, too. Three days later, the mother's bowel burst. If this had happened during the birth, there's a good chance it would have meant the death of mother, baby, or both. The woman's husband, till then an agnostic, came to faith in Jesus Christ.

So God's healing grace comes in a rich variety of ways, sometimes immediate, but always unfolding. I admit that there have been times when feelings of inadequacy have come back, but they have never been overwhelming or debilitating, nor have they lingered as they did. My damaged receiving mechanism is being powerfully healed.

GRACE AND LOVE

Let's return again to the first line of the Prayer Covenant: "Dear Father, thank you for your grace that has made me one of your dearly loved children." This is the foundation for all that follows. Until we have some sense that we are his dearly loved children, we are not ready to move on in prayer.

Well, that's an overstatement. I do want you to pray the rest of the prayer, no matter where you are in your journey, but you get my point. Knowing that God loves you is essential and releases the spirit of prayer. Scripture tells us that God is love (1 John 4:8). And, get this: God is the all-powerful shaping hand behind all that happens in his world. This means that whether you know it or not, even in the painful times, God is working through all that happens to you because he loves you. Of course, for many painful reasons, this is hard to believe. But it is true. And once we believe it, nothing is ever the same. James Bryan Smith writes, "A man in a psychiatrist's office was overheard saying, 'Make me sure that there is a God of love and I shall go away a well man.' His cry is the cry of all of us; make us sure that there is a God of love. It is what we desire most, even if we do not have the words to express it."[2]

The apostle Paul struggled with the thorn in his flesh and pleaded for the Lord to take it away. In his prayers he received these words: "My grace is sufficient for you, for my power is made perfect in weakness" (2 Corinthians 12:9). From then on Paul saw even his trials, of which he had many, as a gift to be received and celebrated, because they sprung from God's gracious love. Paul knew that God forms our character through difficult times.

Paul not only wrote to the churches, he prayed for them; it takes prayer power to grasp this divine, inexhaustible love of Christ. At the heart of his letter to the church of Ephesus he prays that "you, being rooted and established in love, may have power, together with all the saints, to grasp how wide and long and high and deep is the love of Christ" (Ephesians 3:17-18). This love is so great that we can only know it by prayer; and so we pray.

2 (James Bryan Smith, *Embracing the Love of God* [New York: HarperCollins, 1995], p. 3).

No one can fully understand or describe this love of God. It is like standing on a sandy beach in the Carolinas and trying to understand and describe the immensity of the ocean. It is like standing atop a mountain in Colorado, gazing at the Milky Way, and trying to understand the immensity of our galaxy far beyond to the billions of other galaxies in the universe. Richard Foster writes, "If I know, really know, that God loves me, everything is changed. I am no longer a trifling speck in a meaningless cosmos. I am an eternal creature of infinite worth living in a universe animated by love and care and friendship."[3]

Our human capacity and perspective are inadequate to fully understand God's love. The best description I have ever read apart from Scripture comes from the hymn "The Love of God" by Frederick Lehman. The stanza that most deeply speaks to me is this:

Could we with ink the ocean fill,

And were the sky of parchment made,

Were every stalk on earth a quill

And every man a scribe by trade,

To write the love of God above

Would drain the ocean dry,

Nor could the scroll contain the whole

Though stretched from sky to sky.

I love this verse. It paints an accurate picture of the magnitude of God's magnificent love. If every person, man, woman, boy, and girl, over seven billion of us, were to seek to put into words how much God loves each one of us, even though all the oceans were made

---

3 (Richard Foster, (James Bryan Smith, *Embracing the Love of God*, p. xiv).

of ink to supply their pens, they would drain the oceans completely, and even then they would have only just begun.

I can see the image of the quill pen that was used by our founding fathers when they signed the Declaration of Independence. Can you imagine how much a person could write with such a pen and a bottle of ink? Now think how many times we could fill that pen and how many bottles of ink could be filled with the contents of one ocean. That's a lot! Have you ever flown over the Atlantic or Pacific oceans at over five hundred miles an hour, going for hours without seeing land? And can you imagine how deep the water is?

Sure, the verse is a poetic description of God's love, but it is not an exaggeration. God loves you and me that much. "As the Father has loved me, so have I loved you" (John 15:9). God's love is a forgiving love and a personal love. God's love is a perfect love. It is an accepting love. It is an eternal and sacrificial love, and a transforming love. God's love is so great, so profound, and yet so simple. Reporters once asked the great theologian Karl Barth what was the most profound thought he had come across in all his theological studies. His famous reply: "Jesus loves me this I know, for the Bible tells me so."

THE CONTINUING LOVE OF GOD

Sometimes we think God only loved us once. We think of his love as a historical fact—"God so *loved* the world" (John 3:16)—not a present reality. I wrote my master's thesis in theology on Søren Kierkegaard. He wrote a beautiful prayer about God loving us that helps expand our perceptions.

You have loved us first, O God, alas! We speak of it in terms of history as if you loved us but a single time, rather than that without ceasing. When we wake up in the morning and turn our soul toward you—You are there first—You have loved us first; if I rise at dawn and at that same second turn my soul toward You in prayer, You are there ahead of me, You have loved me first. When I withdraw from the distractions of the day and turn my soul toward You, You are there first and forever. And we speak ungratefully as if You have loved us first only once.[4]

Others besides me have been inspired and enriched through this prayer. James Bryan Smith writes, "I had understood God's love as something historical, something that had happened once, but Kierkegaard's prayer taught me that God's love is constant, ever-present and unchanging. Every moment of every day God is with me, loving me first"[5]. Yes! Yes! Yes!

It is all about the love of God. Richard Foster wrote,

The most wonderful thing that can happen to any human is to be loved. It alone speaks to the gnawing insignificance and isolation we feel. And the marvelous news is that we have been loved and we are loved, each and every one us. Uniquely and individually. At the heart of the universe is love, divine love, personal, intimate God-love for you and me. We are known! We are chosen! We are loved! Once experienced at the deepest levels of the soul, no reality can be more profoundly disturbing, more radically healing, more utterly transforming.[6]

---

4 (Richard J. Foster and James Bryan Smith, *Devotional Classics* [San Francisco: Harper SanFrancisco, 1993], 107).

5 (James Bryan Smith, *Embracing the Love of God*, pp. 13-14)

6 (foreword to James Bryan Smith, Embracing the Love of God, p. xiii)

I hope that God's always-first love is real for you. It ought to be your experience, because it is true. I am convinced the greatest need, apart from knowing Jesus as Lord, in every person, in every marriage and family and in every congregation, is for people to know how much they are loved by God. His love is the wind beneath our wings. God's love heals our damaged receiving mechanisms.

"Dear Father, thank you for your grace that has made me one of your dearly loved children." For some time I added this line, "Help me receive and celebrate your love and grace again and again this day." We don't need to make that part of the prayer, but we do need to hold on to that truth continuously. God's grace and love is the foundation stone of the entire Prayer Covenant.

REFLECTION QUESTIONS

Chapter 2   Grace

1. I begin chapter 2 by saying that "Love and grace go hand in hand." How do love and grace work in harmony to unleash and empower our spiritual adventure of following Jesus together?

2. It was difficult for Miss California to believe God loved her because her physical beauty stood in her way. Why is it hard for you to believe that God loves you?

3. Whatever the cause, our "damaged receiving mechanisms" make it hard to believe God loves us. How do grace and the power of prayer work together to begin the healing process to our damaged receiving mechanisms?

4. How could remembering on a regular basis that God loves you graciously and unconditionally help you cope with your current life challenges?

5. Søren Kierkegaard wrote that it is essential we move beyond merely thinking that God "*loved...* " (past and singular tense) to understanding that God *loves...* (present and continuing tense). How can this insight enrich your spiritual adventure in prayer?

CHAPTER 3
LOVE

GOD'S GRACE AND LOVE MAKE us his dearly loved children. That gracious transformation alters our priorities forever. Before God made me his dearly loved child, I put myself first. After I knew his grace and love, I wanted to put God first. I have found placing him first to be both a great joy and a continual challenge. That is why the next line of the Prayer Covenant is "By your grace make knowing, loving and obeying you my highest priority." I only recently added this line to the Prayer Covenant, and I can't believe it took me so long! I am eager to tell you about this request and how important it is.

It's really all about loving God. The Great Commandment is "Love the Lord your God with all your heart and with all your soul and with all your mind and with all your strength" (Mark 12:30). But we have so sentimentalized the word love that we need to delve into the Bible to discover what truly loving God means. There are three themes I want to highlight. Loving God means: knowing God, obeying God, and placing God first.

THE PRIORITY OF GOD

"You shall have no other gods before me" (Exodus 20:3). This first commandment was hard for the Israelites to understand. Every other religion had multiple gods, and those multiple gods didn't mind "sharing." You could worship as many or as few of the gods as you liked; it was your choice. However, the God of Israel did mind sharing. Throughout their history the people of Israel were wandering away from God, and he had to send prophets to call them back again and again.

Jesus, like his Father, didn't share. Jesus made it clear that other gods, as well as anything that competes with him for complete and total allegiance, were to be ruled out: "If anyone comes to me and does not hate father and mother, wife and children, brothers and sisters—yes, even their own life—such a person cannot be my disciple. And whoever does not carry their cross and follow me cannot be my disciple" (Luke 14:25-26).

Jesus is claiming priority over everything, even over those we love and hold dear.

I am continually learning what it means to love God by putting him first. In the early 1990s I was traveling on the freeways of Los Angeles listening to a tape by Stephen Covey of the Franklin Covey Day Planner. The message had a powerful impact on me. During his teaching, Covey asked the question, "What is the most important thing in your life?" He declared that it is essential for every person to wrestle that question to the ground. Once you feel confident of your answer to that question, ask yourself, "What is the second most important thing in my life?" Then clarify the third, and the fourth, and the fifth, and so on. Then he said, "This will be the most important list you will ever make in your life." I believe he is right.

Then he said this: "It is worth taking a five-hour retreat to think through your answer to these questions and understand your top priorities." We are all very busy, and it is not easy to set aside five hours, but I believe he is speaking truth. In fact, I have spent well over a hundred hours thinking about and rethinking my answers. It has been preeminently worthwhile.

I knew my answer to the first question immediately because I knew Jesus' response to the lawyer who asked him, "Teacher, which is the greatest commandment in the Law?" Jesus replied: "'Love the Lord your God with all your heart and with all your soul and with all your mind.' This is the first and greatest commandment. And the second is like it: 'Love your neighbor as yourself.' All the Law and the Prophets hang on these two commandments" (Matthew 22:37-40).

Jesus knew what he was talking about. As a follower of Christ, I want my life to be consistent with Jesus' life and teaching, especially on what he thinks is most important. I knew then that I had the right answer, but I wasn't sure whether my life consistently reflected that answer. In fact, as I thought about it, I quickly became aware that my life did not reflect my answer as much I wanted it to. I asked myself, how much was I saying what I thought my answer ought to be? That led to serious reflection then and still does to this day. It is so much easier to know and say the right words than to live by them. But I felt good about my answer and began to think about its meaning and implications.

Confident that I had the right answer about priority number one, I moved on to think about the second most important thing in my life, and the third, and fourth, and fifth. I had not put these priorities in writing before. The whole exercise gave me a greater sense of clarity, energy, and well-being. I believed that in a new way I was doing what Covey said was most important, "making the main thing the main thing." At least I thought so then.

About four weeks later, I was reflecting on Scripture, especially Paul's prayer in his letter to the Ephesians, which you may grow tired of hearing about by the end of this book, but it's so important that I want to keep quoting it:

[I pray] that out of his glorious riches he may strengthen you with power through his Spirit in your inner being, so that Christ may dwell in your hearts through faith. And I pray that you, being rooted and established in love, may have power, together with all the saints, to grasp how wide and long and high and deep is the love of Christ, and to know this love that surpasses knowledge—that you may be filled to the measure of all the fullness of God. (Ephesians 3:16-19)

I wanted to be filled with "all the fullness of God." I wanted to know the rich dimensions of Christ's love for me, if that was the key to "the fullness of God." That led me to ponder my former answer to the question "What is the most important thing in my life?" Love for God is the great commandment. But is that the most important thing in my life? Is there something even more important than love for God? Is there something that precedes love for God, that produces love for God, and that inspires worship of and obedience to God? Yes, there is! It is God's love for us. God's love for us is even more important than our love for God, because our love is a response to his love.

Wow! It was like a lightbulb turning on in my head—a life-changing thought. It opened the floodgates of grace and joy and love and energy. My heart is inspired to worship because God loves us first. God's love sent Jesus into the world and into my life. God's love inspired Jesus' birth, and Jesus' obedient love led him to the cross. No doubt, God's redeeming love is more important than my love for him.

Awe filled my heart. This dawning of God's first love for me produced in me even deeper strength and freedom. The riches of this insight continue to unfold. The more I allow God's love for me to fill my life, the more I appreciate and love him. "I will praise you, O Lord, with all my heart!" His love sets me free to love myself. This may sound strange, but it is true. The more I love myself in response to his love, the more I am set free to love him and to love others.

So I knew, then, the main thing. The main thing is not what I do but what God does. He loves. He forgives. He redeems. He heals. He inspires. He reconciles. He transforms. He establishes our relationship through the person of Jesus on the basis of his saving grace. This is what keeps the Prayer Covenant from being a burden, just another form of legalism. He lifts us up and sets us free to love lavishly. Once I knew the highest priority, I wanted to shout it everywhere. This is the gospel! This is good news! The apostle John describes God's love for us and finally concludes, "God is love" (1 John 4:8). He doesn't just love us. He is love, and His love changes everything. "We love because he first loved us" (1 John 4:19).

GETTING DOWN TO THE MAIN THING

Some weeks later, I was thinking about God's goodness, mercy, faithfulness, love, and on and on. I was feeling a bit self-righteous and smug about my discovery, and then it dawned on me like a bolt of lightning. Oh my! How could this be? I realized my answer to the question "What was the most important thing in my life?" had still missed the mark. Why do I keep thinking about things?

God's love for me is more important than my love for God, and it is the place to start in the Prayer Covenant. But I concluded it must not be the most important thing in my life. There was something far more important than God's love for me. I wondered how I missed it. It is so obvious. I had gone to seminary. I had pastored and preached for nearly thirty years. I had known the Lord and followed him passionately for more than forty years. By this time, I had taken nearly one hundred hours to think about the most important things in my life. How could I have missed the highest priority? When the answer is so simple and so clear in Scripture again and again, how could I miss it for so long?

But before going on, I have a question for you. What is more important than God's love for you? I urge you to stop reading now and attempt to answer that question for yourself before you read my answer. Seriously, I hope you will stop reading now and think about what is more important than God's love for you. I believe you will agree with my answer. But it matters far more to me that you think through your answer for yourself before you read my answer. I don't want you to miss the blessing of thinking deeply about this. The answer to this question ought to change everything. If you come up with the true answer on your own, it will mean far more to you and those around you. And if you work diligently to clarify your answer but choose a lesser priority, you will still think about and possibly embrace what I believe is the true answer much more passionately.

Do you agree with Stephen Covey and with me that it is worth a five-hour retreat for you to think through what is the most important thing in your life? And then what is the second most important? Third, and fourth, and fifth, and so on? Do you know what your priorities in life are? Or what you believe they should be? Are those priorities carefully and comprehensively articulated, truly guiding your life decisions and time commitments? How consistently does your life reflect those priorities? How deeply do you want your life to do so? I had to face all these questions for myself and still do. If you answer them for yourself, you will be glad you did.

Once more, I urge you to stop reading, set the book down, and give serious attention to answering these questions for yourself. It will be waiting for you when you come back. Or are you satisfied with merely evaluating my answer and then seeing if you agree with it? Do you believe that this is the most important list you will ever make? If so, is it not worth your time to wrestle your answers to the ground?

MY FINAL ANSWER

Did you do it? If not, this is your last opportunity to stop reading and seek to clarify your own answers before learning mine, because in the next sentence I'm going to tell you my answer.

Of course! How could I have missed it? The one thing more important than God's love for me and my love for God is God himself.

God himself is infinitely more important than anything he does. The eternal Almighty God, Father, Son, and Holy Spirit, is far more important than his love, his goodness, his faithfulness, his grace, or his mercy. How could I have missed it?

How much do I reflect on God himself compared to what God has done, does, or what I hope he will do? For nearly forty years, I had only learned verses 9 and 11 of Psalm 119. I had memorized both but had skipped verse 10. Psalm 119:9 says, "How can a young person stay on the path of purity? By living according to your word." Verse 11 says, "I have hidden your word in my heart that I might not sin against you." My focus from these verses had been on purity and obedience. Then I memorized verse 10: "I will seek you with all my heart; do not let me stray from your commandments." The first half of this verse is the key to all three verses: "I will seek you with all my heart."

The Psalms provide glimpses into those who desired and knew God in the Old Testament. David writes, "One thing I ask of the LORD, this is what I seek: that I may dwell in the house of the LORD all the days of my life; to gaze upon the beauty of the LORD and to seek him in his temple" (Psalm 27:4). In another psalm he says, "My soul thirsts for God, for the living God. When can I go and meet with God?" (Psalm 42:2). In Psalm 63:1-2 we read, "O, God, you are my God, earnestly I seek you; I thirst for you, my body longs for you, in a dry and weary land where there is no water." There is power released when we focus on the Lord himself, when we commune with him and worship him.

The deepest issue I must face, that we all must face, is whether in our hearts and minds we actually do place God first. Do I really love him and seek him with all my heart? Really? Or am I more attracted to, enthralled by, and impressed with what God does for me and through me? Has working for God become my god? Where is my attention? Am I focused on God himself, or mostly on what God does?

KNOWING GOD

Loving God by placing him first means I am engaged in the adventure of knowing God. I will be discovering what it means to know God, more and more and better and better, throughout my life and eternity. God created us to love us. He created us for fellowship. He redeems us as his sons and daughters for fellowship. God wants us to know him. In Genesis 3:8-9 we read "Then the man and his wife heard the sound of the LORD God as he was walking in the garden in the cool of the day, and they hid from the LORD God among the trees of the garden. But the LORD God called to the man, 'Where are you?'"

This is Adam and Eve's first encounter with God after they had betrayed him and decided to trust the Serpent instead. The impression I get from reading this passage is that God showed up regularly for an afternoon walk in the Garden with Adam and Eve. He wanted to be with them, to enjoy them, and to let them enjoy being with him. Of course now, after their disobedience, Adam and Eve were no longer comfortable with the presence of God; they are hiding in the bushes—which is where the whole human race has been ever since. God calls them out of the bushes, and he has been calling all Adam and Eve's children out of the bushes ever since.

Not surprisingly, Jesus makes knowing God the central focus of his Last Supper prayer, which commentators call his High Priestly Prayer. "Now this is eternal life: that they know you, the only true God, and Jesus Christ, whom you have sent" (John 17:3). What could be clearer than this? What is more important than eternal life and knowing God? And what is more important than Jesus Christ, who is the way to the truth and the knowledge of God?

The apostle Paul believed that knowing God in Jesus Christ was not only essential, but also it was the driving motivation of his life:

I want to know Christ—yes, to know the power of his resurrection and participation in his sufferings, becoming like him in his death, and so, somehow, attaining to the resurrection from the dead. Not that I have already obtained all this, or have already arrived at my goal, but I press on to take hold of that for which Christ Jesus took hold of me. Brothers and sisters, I do not consider myself yet to have taken hold of it. But one thing I do: forgetting what is behind and straining toward what is ahead, I press on toward the goal to win the prize for which God has called me heavenward in Christ Jesus. (Philippians 3:10-14)

This passage from Philippians was the one I used when preparing for the celebration of our fiftieth wedding anniversary. I wanted to share it with our twenty-eight grandkids for two reasons: I wanted them to understand the priority of knowing God in Jesus Christ, and I wanted them to know that through Christ they would find their destiny in life and eternity. I wanted them to know how deeply their lives matter to God.

Ironically, this special event led to the most embarrassing moment of my life. During my entire talk to my grandchildren at our fiftieth wedding anniversary, I didn't even mention my wife, Patty! Some weeks later she quietly and graciously pointed out this oversight. Ouch! God is first, and must be first, but Patty is the love of my life. I regret that I didn't honor her as I should have. I have dedicated this book to her so that I may speak now for all to know. We have had a wonderful life of knowing God, following Jesus together, and nurturing our family of over sixty people.

In contrast to the biblical priority of knowing God, the world today is so self-centered. We are encouraged in so many ways to think "it's all about me." How greatly we build our lives thinking about and looking out for ourselves: my desires, my dreams, my family, my body, my appearance, how I impress people.

One of my greatest encouragements in seeking to know God comes from a favorite author of mine. He was not a theologian or scholar, but instead a humble kitchen worker in a seventeenth-century monastery. Brother Lawrence described his experience of being with God:

> I think it's proper to inform you after what manner I consider myself before God whom I behold as my king. I consider myself as the most wretched of men who has committed all sorts of crimes against his king. Touched with a sensible regret I confess to him all my wickedness. I ask his forgiveness. I abandon myself in his hands, that he may do what he pleases with me. The king, full of mercy and goodness, very far from chastising me, embracing me with love, makes me eat at his table, serves me with his own hands, gives me the key of his treasure; he converses and delights himself with me incessantly in a thousand and thousand ways, and treats me in all respects as his favorite.[7]

Whoever we are, wherever we are, it is a joy and pleasure to know God, now and for eternity.

OBEYING GOD

Knowing God is about a relationship with God, a loving relationship—

---

7 (Brother Lawrence, *Practicing the Presence of God*, A Spire Book, Jove Publications for Fleming H. Revell, Old Tappan, NJ: 1958], p. 26).

and as Adam and Eve discovered, a loving relationship with God is kept alive through obedience. It is no surprise that through Moses God instructed his chosen people:

> Hear, O Israel: The LORD our God, the LORD is one. Love the LORD your God with all your heart and with all your soul and with all your strength. These commandments that I give you today are to be on your hearts. Impress them on your children. Talk about them when you sit at home and when you walk along the road, when you lie down and when you get up. Tie them as symbols on your hands and bind them on your foreheads. Write them on the doorframes of your houses and on your gates. (Deuteronomy 6:4-9)

Notice in this passage that loving and obeying God go hand in hand. It is common for people to say that the Old Testament is about commandments and the New Testament is about love; this is a mistake. In the preceding passage, love and the commandments are spoken of together.

Jesus teaches the priority of love, too. I quoted this verse at the beginning of the chapter, and now I want to quote it again" "Love the Lord your God with all your heart and with all your soul and with all your mind and with all your strength" (Mark 12:30).

Jesus repeatedly connects love and obedience. He tells the disciples on the night before he is to be crucified, "If you love me, keep my commands" (John 14:15). This is direct and pointed. Jesus requires his disciples to obey him. That includes you and me. Yet, this commandment of Jesus is not the pronouncement of a tyrant—Jesus wants his disciples to experience what is best, which is to love and to live in love. He elaborates, "If you keep my commands, you will remain in my love, just as I have kept my

Father's commands and remain in his love" (John 15:10). I am eager to stay in the love of Jesus. I don't want to be outside the shining light of his love for even a minute.

Andrew Murray, in his book *With Christ in the School of Prayer*, captures this biblical priority of loving obedience when he says:

> Obedience is the only path that leads to the glory of God. Obedience doesn't replace or supply its shortcomings. But faith's obedience gives access to all the blessings that God has for us. In the Gospel of John, the baptism of the Spirit (John 14:16), the manifestation of the Son (John14:21), the indwelling of the Father (John 14:23), the abiding in Christ's love (John 15:10), the privilege of his holy friendship (John 15:14), and the power of effective prayer (John15:16), all wait for the obedience.[8]

Murray calls for this obedience at the beginning of every day: "Our first thought should be: 'I belong to the master.' Every moment I must act as his property, as part of himself, as one who only seeks to know and do his will. I am a servant, a slave of Jesus Christ. Let this be the spirit that animates me"[9] (ibid., p. 173).

Loving obedience is at the heart of Christian discipleship. At one time this link between love and obedience in the Bible made me wonder: does this mean that God's love is conditional, that he only loves us if we obey him? You will, no doubt, have run into people who manipulate by means of love. "If you really loved me you would... buy me an ice cream cone... buy me a car... let me

---

8 (Andrew Murray, *With Christ in the School of Prayer* [Springdale, PA: Whitaker House, 1981], pp. 172-73).
9 (ibid., p. 173).

do what I want . . ." That conditional and manipulative expression of love is not what goes on with God. God loves us. Period. He is love. Everything he does is motivated by his love. He requires us to love him because he knows that only by loving and obeying him can we be all that he created us to be. It is because God loves us that he wants us to obey him. In response to God's love, we show that we love him by obeying.

There were those in the first-century church who tried to separate love and obedience. One of the primary reasons for the letter of 1 John was to confront and correct this thinking. To those who were saying that they were free to do whatever they wanted because of God's grace in Christ, he says, in effect, "Not so fast." On the contrary, he writes, "In fact, this is love for God: to keep his commands. And his commands are not burdensome" (1 John 5:3).

Keeping love and obedience together was not just a challenge for those Christians in the first century. In the first part of the twentieth century there were many earnest Christians who taught that every Christian could accept Jesus as their Savior, and then only really dedicated Christians went beyond salvation to discipleship—Jesus could be your Savior, and then later on he could be your Lord.

I am confident this is not what Jesus teaches. In his Great Commission to the disciples, Jesus makes obedience central to their task of mission:

> Then Jesus came to them and said, "All authority in heaven and on earth has been given to me. Therefore go and make disciples of all nations, baptizing them in the name of the Father and of the Son and of the Holy Spirit, and teaching them to obey everything I have commanded you. And surely I am with you always, to the very end of the age." (Matthew 28:18-20)

Tying together salvation and discipleship, I like to say it this way; "We are saved by faith alone. But the faith that saves is never alone. Jesus saves those over whom he is Lord." If Jesus is your Lord, you can trust he is your Savior. If you do not desire Jesus to be your Lord, it is questionable that he is your Savior. The most pressing question we can ask ourselves is "Is Jesus my Lord?" We will explore the lordship of Jesus Christ throughout this book, especially in chapter seven when we consider what it means to pray "Jesus, be Lord of my life today in new ways, and change me any way you want."

CONCLUSION

Love God. Make God first. Give yourself completely and totally to him. The fruit that comes from this total commitment is totally wonderful.

> Give up yourself, and you will find your real self. Lose your life and you will save it. Submit to death, death of your ambitions and favourite wishes every day and the death of your whole body in the end; submit with every fibre of your being, and you will find eternal life. Keep back nothing. Nothing that you have not given away will be really yours. Nothing in you that has not died will ever be raised from the dead. Look for yourself, and you will find in the long run only hatred, loneliness, despair, rage, ruin and decay. But look for Christ and you will find Him, and with Him everything else thrown in.[10]

Of course, now that we have explored the necessity of giving first

---

10 (C. S. Lewis, *Mere Christianity* (New York, HarperCollins, 2001), p. 248).

place to God and the benefits that come from it, we must stop—even come to a screeching halt! You can't do this on your own. You can't put God first. If you try in your own strength, you are doomed to frustration. It is the character of the fallen nature to place ourselves first. It is impossible in our current condition to put God first. That's why we must make this second line of the Prayer Covenant our impassioned request. This is why we begin this line, "By your grace . . ."

Now, having prayed for grace to make God first, we go on to explore what we next need to pray for, that God would empower us to love others as he loves us.

REFLECTION QUESTIONS

Chapter 3 • Love

1. Loving God should be the focus of our lives and spring from God's grace and the depths of our hearts. How would you rate yourself as a lover of God?

2. Loving God is a challenge to the ordering of our lives and our life-priorities. What are your life-priorities? How do you see these priorities expressed in your daily patterns and practices?

3. What do you need to do to set aside a significant block of time, perhaps three to five hours, to evaluate and order your life-priorities?

4. Loving God includes seeking to know him. What are you doing to know him and know him better than you do?

5. Loving God also requires that we obey him. What reservations do you have about total obedience? What areas of your life—what relationships, career goals, possessions, etc., do you need to bring under his lordship?

CHAPTER 4
COMPASSION

THE THIRD LINE OF THE Prayer Covenant is: "Empower me to love others the way you love me." This request follows naturally from the first and second. We want to know God's love, and then we respond back to God with love, and then we want to share it with others. This line is entitled "Compassion" because we are praying to share God's love with others in the challenges and joys of life. Sharing God's love in the daily rough-and-tumble of life is one of the great privileges of following Jesus together. We hurt with others and we celebrate with others, all in Jesus' name.

Love begets love. Love comes to us from the outside before it is inside us. It is because we have received God's love that we can share it with others. I know this is true, because I was loved as a child and young person and as a result was able to receive the love of Christ through others and then share it. I think of my parents, Young Life, and my local congregation on Queen Anne Hill in Seattle who loved me. First and foremost, my parents loved me, and I knew it. My mother spent the vast majority of her last five months of pregnancy on the couch in order to carry me to full term. Mom and Dad often reminded me of that as a way of saying to me how much they wanted me and loved me.

As a student, my Young Life leaders loved me. Add Sewell, one of the four founders of Young Life, as well as young people who were coming to faith in Christ in Seattle, reached out to me in love. Mike McCutchen was a key person. At that time he was one of the outstanding basketball players in Seattle and later in the country while playing at the University of Washington. With him I became part of the leadership training group and found strong love and support through other volunteer leaders of clubs in Seattle high schools.

Because I was experiencing God's love in Jesus, I wanted to share it, and so founded a Young Life club my sophomore year at Bothell High School. Through the power of God many students came to the Lord and were open to grow in their faith under my leadership. When I saw their transformation by the message and love of Christ, I was encouraged and strengthened to give myself more deeply. I spent five summers at Young Life camps in Colorado with gifted staff, immersed and surrounded by those who loved the Lord and who loved young people sacrificially. Every week I saw young people come to know Jesus Christ as their Savior and Lord and begin a new life. It was amazing!

THE WAY THAT GOD LOVES

We have all kinds of ideas about love: we have songs, poems, novels, and movies, and some are better than others. What do the Scriptures have to say about love? The Old Testament uses two primary words for love. What both words convey is that God's love is the kind that doesn't fluctuate, break, or cease but builds an unbreakable bond. Hosea, the prophet of God's love, wrote, "I led them with cords of human kindness, with ties of love; I lifted the yoke from their neck, and bent down to feed them" (Hosea 11:4). This kind of love is not natural to us; we must pray for it. "Empower me to love others the way you love me."

The Greeks had four words for love. The word for love most used in the New Testament is agape. It accentuates what is unique about the love of God—that God's love is self-initiating and self-generating. God loves, not because we are lovely, inspiring, or deserving, but because it is his nature to love. This is the word for love used by Jesus in his final instructions to his disciples, a passage we discussed in the previous chapter: "A new command I give you: Love one another. As I have loved you, so you must love one another. By this everyone will know that you are my disciples, if you love one another" (John 13:34-35).

Following the pattern of Jesus' life, love is more than a feeling; love includes action. "At just the right time, when we were still powerless, Christ died for the ungodly. Very rarely will anyone die for a righteous man, though for a good man someone might possibly dare to die. But God demonstrates his own love (*agape*) for us in this: While we were still sinners, Christ died for us" (Romans 5:6-8). The love God commands in us expresses itself in actions. What can we do for those we have been called to love that will be helpful and bless them? Sometimes we may have to act before we feel love. Sometimes we may act and never feel. It is certainly best when we act and we feel. This kind of love, too, is not natural to us; we must pray for it. "Empower me love others the way you love me."

Jesus is not merely *feeling* love for his disciples; he loves them and is acting out his love for them. He determined to love his first disciples, and us, at the cost of his life. He chose to love. This is what Jesus wants us to do with fellow believers, and our families and friends. He wants us to choose them. This kind of love involves our mind, our will and our emotions.

I apply this commandment in all kinds of ways. One of the ways I express the Lord's love is to use the phone. I love to call dear brothers and sisters in Christ with no other agenda except to find out how they are doing. They are surprised and blessed. Just today I called a woman who was in severe pain last week to find out if she was still in pain and to pray with her. She thanked me for following up on our conversation. People love to know that someone cares, that someone is thinking about them and praying for them, that they are not following Jesus alone.

There is such joy in time spent on the phone, not doing business or working on a project, but just showing and sharing the love of the Lord. People know that God loves them, but often they need love with "skin on it." Another way I seek to share the Lord's love is to pray for people. I have been in thousands of Prayer Covenants over the years. There is no greater joy than praying the Prayer Covenant over those whom I love and who love me in the Lord.

THE WELCOMING LOVE OF GOD

God's compassionate love in Jesus Christ is welcoming and forgiving. I love this story about the towels and the tree limbs because it illustrates so well this dynamic of God's love.

There was a young man who was rebellious, hard to raise, and involved with drugs. He left home at sixteen because he despised his parents and refused to honor or obey them. After five or six years he realized he had made a terrible mistake and wrote a letter seeking reconciliation.

He gathered what resources he had and boarded a train for home without knowing whether he would be received. The closer he got to his hometown, the more anxious he became. A woman sitting across the aisle noticed and asked if she could be helpful. He told her his story. Since his home was next to the train tracks he had written to his parents, "If you are open to my coming home, put a towel on the lower limb of the tree closest to the tracks. If you do, I will see it from the train and get off at the next station. If you don't, I will understand and just keep going." Then he told her, "The closer I get to the house, the more anxious I am becoming."

"How about if I watch at the window for you; I will let you know what I see," volunteered the woman. When the train came around the curve and the tree became visible, the woman was shocked. She said to him, "I can see the tree. There is a towel on every limb. Welcome home! They can hardly wait to see you."

This story of the towels is a variation on Jesus' parable of the prodigal son in Luke 15. There was a young man who went to his wealthy father and demanded his share of the family inheritance. The young man was basically saying to his father, "I can't wait for you to die. Give me now what I will get after you do." What could be more insulting and painful than that? Worse, this demand would have been known throughout the entire community and would have been a source of great shame. Despite the insult, rejection, and shame, the father sold off enough of the family homestead to give his younger son the cash he demanded. Then the young man headed out into foreign lands, squandering the money and becoming destitute. He ended up with the most demeaning job for a Jewish boy—feeding the pigs. He was so hungry that he wanted to eat what he was feeding the pigs. That is pretty desperate. It dawned on him that the family servants from his home had a better life than he was living. He decided to return home, not as a son, but asking to be reinstated merely as a servant.

What is wonderfully touching about this story as Jesus tells it: the father saw the son coming from a long way off and ran to meet him. Evidently the father had been watching for his son. Running was not something a dignified patriarch did in that society, yet Jesus portrays the father as lifting up his robe and running to his son. Very undignified! The wayward son was welcomed home. No mention is given of the insults, shame, or squandered money. Instead the father said, "Quick! Bring the best robe and put it on him. Put a ring on his finger and sandals on his feet. Bring the fattened calf and kill it. Let's have a feast and celebrate. For this son of mine was dead and is alive again; he was lost and is found" (Luke 15:22-24). This was full restoration. There is a towel on every limb of the tree.

This portrays the welcoming and forgiving love of God for us, and it is to be the way we welcome and love each other. It is inevitable that others will hurt us, offend us, and inflict all kinds of pain. The way of the world is to reject and exclude the offenders. The way of God's love is to forgive and keep the relationship warm, welcoming, and alive. That is why, despite the scruples of the religious leaders of his day, Jesus embraced prostitutes, lepers, tax collectors, and other outcasts of his society. God calls us to love others by embracing those whom we have good reasons to reject. Our calling is to have lots of towels and to be sure they are on every limb of the tree. Who do you know who is fearful that there will not be a towel on the tree for them?

While this request of the Prayer Covenant flows out of the first one, it has not been a part of the Prayer for most of my life. I have only recently come to see how essential it is that we receive the love of God and then pray for help to share that love with others. That damaged receiving mechanism of ours needs a lot of prayer to be healed. And so it is with everyone you know.

The apostle Paul prayed that the love of God would flow into the churches to which he wrote. I want to return again to the passage in Ephesians:

> For this reason I kneel before the Father, from whom every family in heaven and on earth derives its name. I pray that out of his glorious riches he may strengthen you with power through his Spirit in your inner being, so that Christ may dwell in your hearts through faith. And I pray that you, being rooted and established in love, may have power, together with all the saints, to grasp how wide and long and high and deep is the love of Christ, and to know this love that surpasses knowledge—that you may be filled to the measure of all the fullness of God. (Ephesians 3:14-19)

Paul prayed for the riches of Christ's love to indwell the Ephesians. From this we can see that love is not something we generate from ourselves, but it is something of God that he shares with us. God is love and God loves us. He fills us with love. Once we have been filled up with love, then it can overflow from our lives into the lives of others. An elderly member of my family quoted an unknown author, "I'm drinking from my saucer because my cup is overflowing." If we think love is something we must dredge up from somewhere deep inside, we are on a hopeless quest that will only lead to frustration. That is why we pray to be empowered to love others the way that he loves us. True love doesn't come from us, but it does come through us.

LOVED INTO BECOMING LOVING

Years ago I heard this story from Zig Ziglar and I have never forgotten it. The story has been told and retold a number of times by others to make different points. The point that I want to make from the story is that the more we know how much God loves us, the more we love ourselves and the more we are able to love others.

In one of the tribal cultures of Africa, when a young man wanted to marry, he was required to provide a dowry to the father. Usually the dowry was one cow. The more gifted and attractive the woman, the more likely the dowry would become two cows. There was one woman who was considered homely by most, but one man was deeply in love with her. She wasn't ugly, but calling her plain would definitely be a compliment. She was skinny and walked with her shoulders hunched and her head ducked. Her father was afraid he wouldn't be able to marry her off at all. When the groom-to-be announced the engagement, he gave the father ten cows as a dowry. The father was shocked by the request to marry and by the size of the dowry. Now, instead of being stuck with her, he had received ten cows for her.

In that culture the honeymoon was for two years. When the couple returned, her father saw her at a distance and was shocked. She was beautiful. The lift of her shoulders, the tilt of her chin, the sparkle in her eyes, her dress and hair—all spelled self-confidence and pride. It was not an arrogant and haughty pride but a confident inner beauty that radiated in her every movement. She was stunning.

The father ran to his daughter. "Honey, what has happened to you?" he asked in delightful surprise. "You are beautiful."

"I am not the same woman I was. I did not know I was a ten-cow woman," she replied. "That is, until my husband believed I was, until my husband told me I was, and until my husband treated me as though I was." When we receive compassion and love we are made whole. We are set free to love and have compassion for others.

That is the way of God toward us. He made the world for us. He brought us into the world. He sent his Son to rescue us from spiritual brokenness and captivity. He tells us we are of supreme value. When we know how much he loves us, we are able to enter into love. It surrounds us. It fills us. It overflows from us.

It is the lavish love of God that makes you loveable when you thought you were a one-cow person. We are damaged goods. Each of us needs to know and remember that God says we are each a ten-cow person, and he treats us that way. This changes everything. When we know we are loved and discover that we are loveable, we become loving.

It was a similar truth that touched coach, Bill McCartney, the founder of Promise Keepers, and which led him to resign from coaching the University of Colorado football team. A visiting preacher was talking about the special calling of a husband to so love his wife that she would know how special she was. "If you are loving her the way God has called you to love her you will see splendor in her eyes and not torment. You will see contentment and not anguish."

Coach McCartney did not see that splendor nor that contentment. Two days later he had the courage to resign from coaching and dedicate his life to his dear wife and family, and to Promise Keepers. Thank you Coach for Christian character, your example and the impact of Promise Keepers on our nation.

LOVE IS FOR THE BIRDS

Birds have become special to my knowing and sharing the love of God. In the early 1980s I was pastoring College Hill Presbyterian Church with that incredible staff, a strong board of elders, and a congregation that believed that ministry belongs to the people of God, not just professional clergy. They inspired and encouraged me to follow Christ as Lord and to be filled with his Spirit. I have often said that they loved me into wholeness and prayed me into fruitfulness.

Doris Trabert Marsh was the widow of Marc Trabert and later of Charles Marsh, both of whom were dear friends to me and strong followers of Christ. One day Doris came to see me in my office and told me of her love for birds and especially cardinals. She told me of having a birdfeeder and buying seeds that attract cardinals, and that every time she would see a cardinal, she would stop and be reminded of these words on the lips of Jesus: "Doris, I love you." Through the suffering she experienced in the deaths of both of her husbands, Marc through a plane crash and Charles through a long bout with cancer, she found comfort and solace through this reminder of God's love every time she saw a cardinal—usually five to ten times each day.

I thought she had a good idea and potentially a great idea. But I had no sense of how the story would affect the rest of my life. I assumed it was worth my doing the same thing to see how God's love and grace could grow within me. I began by buying a birdfeeder and placing it outside my office window. I bought seeds that especially attract cardinals. And every time I saw a cardinal, I would stop and remember these words of Jesus: "Jerry, I love you." I would often see six to eight cardinals each day. It was a wonderful reminder throughout the day that God's love was real and fresh and powerful. It kept me on the alert to see a cardinal.

One morning I came to the top of the hill across from my home where I would go regularly to pray. I was blessed to see a beautiful red cardinal flying from a tree on the left, across fifty yards of lawn, to a tree on the right, and I was reminded of God's love in Christ for me. After the cardinal landed on a lower limb of the tree, it flew to another limb, and I again thanked God for his love. I kept watching, and every time it flew to another limb or another tree, I was reminded of God's love: "Jerry, I love you." I was exploding inside with gratitude and then with joy. By the time that cardinal left my sight, I found myself reflecting on the love of God in new ways. And I realized in a much deeper way that he wanted to love others through me so they could know of his love for them.

It was good. In fact, it was more than good. It was great. It was true. It was life nurturing and challenging. And then this thought came to me: "If God told me he loved me every time he wanted me to know his love, it wouldn't be just when I saw a cardinal. It would be much more than that." So I decided I would use the reminder of seeing any bird to speak to me of God's love. "Jerry, I love you. Jerry, I love you. Jerry, I love you." This one simple decision changed everything. Now I wasn't reminded of God's love six to eight times a day. I was reminded of his love from my side porch and the hill across the street fifty to seventy-five times each morning during my time alone with God.

Then I would go to my office and would be reminded again of God's love between twenty-five and a hundred times every day. For some time, I began with those same words: "Jerry, I love you." Then I moved to just saying, "Thank you, Lord. Thank you, Father." And each time I would do it, a sense of being loved, of well-being, a spirit of thankfulness and joy were released within me.

I've been doing this for over twenty years. I have been reminded of the love of God every day. I've been reminded of the love of

God many, many times during the day. I have remembered and received his love intentionally, repeatedly, concretely, hundreds of thousands of times since 1990.

Can you imagine what has happened to my "receiving mechanism"? It is being healed continually. God tells me I am one of his "dearly loved children." In Christ, we are the beloved of God. This is the truth. This is the truth of God for me and for you. It is good news, God's good news.

I am thankful to Doris Trabert Marsh for bringing into my life a window into the love of God for me, and the love of God through me to others. I share this story everywhere I can because I don't know anyone who doesn't need more of God's love. Do you? God's purpose is to continually fill our love bank that we can continually make deposits of that love to all we know.

LOVE TRIGGERS

For many years, I was part of a covenant group of pastors and theologians, and we would spend three days together each year. One year, one of the brothers said to the group, "Every time I see a cardinal, I say to myself, 'God loves Jerry.'" Everybody laughed. But then I said, "No! No! No! Don't say that. I hope that every time you see a cardinal or any bird, you will be reminded of how much God loves you, what that love cost him and what that love enables us to do."

The point is this: We all need a regular trigger that reminds us of God's love for us. You choose the trigger that works for you. For me, it has been birds, because I see so many of them every day. For Mother Teresa, the trigger was seeing someone in need. Whenever she saw someone in need, she saw an opportunity to serve Jesus in that person from the message of Matthew 25, and her deepest desire was to minister to Jesus. Listen to her words:

> Jesus is my God, Jesus is my spouse and Jesus is my life. Jesus is my only love, Jesus is my all and Jesus is my everything. Because of this I am never afraid. I am doing my work with Jesus. I am doing it for Jesus. I am doing it to Jesus; therefore, the results are his, not mine.[11]

I want to love Jesus the way that she loved Jesus. I have tried to use her approach but I haven't been able to make it work for me. Choose what works best for you. But pick some trigger that reminds you every day repeatedly of how much God loves you and intends to love others through you.

Some years ago, I had a cataract operation, and it has produced floaters in one of my eyes. Because of those floaters, I can see birds even when they aren't there. But I am always looking for birds. I can easily see them a block or two away. We have the lawns of six houses behind our home, and I am able to see beyond those lawns and trees to three blocks away. And I have developed this habit of receiving the love of God so often and for so long that now all I need to do is to look up at the sky, and I am reminded of the love of God even when there are no birds flying, because I know birds were there. And when I hear birds sing, I know what they are singing; do you? Before I get out of bed during the summer I hear their songs early in the morning.

---

11 (Mother Teresa, *Jesus Is My All in All: Praying with the 'Saint of Calcutta'* [New York: Doubleday, 2008], p. 10)

Incorporating this into my life also means that I have a big advantage in my golf game. I have a secret weapon. I can be playing poorly, in fact, very poorly. And then I see a bird or a group of birds and am reminded of God's love and I say, "Thank you, Lord." It relaxes me and helps me to stop taking myself and my golf so seriously. It's amazing what that does for my golf game. I feel sorry for those I'm playing with because usually they either don't know or they don't use my secret weapon.

One day I was waiting for my younger son to return to his high school from a golf match and the delay was extensive. I had compressed my schedule and driven quickly to be on time at the high school because I didn't want to hold him up after his long match. After an hour of waiting, with my impatience growing by the minute, a flock of about two hundred birds descended on the circle of grass next to the car and I burst out laughing. I got the message! God loves me and wants to love my son through me. Instantly, the impatience and irritation were gone, and so was the stress. I think my son was surprised by my warm welcome after waiting so long. So was I.

I've been so blessed to have a trigger that reminds me of God's love again and again every day for over twenty years that I have created other triggers as well, although none serve me as well as the birds. When I see raindrops, I'm reminded of God's love because he is refreshing and replenishing the earth. Whenever I see snowflakes, I am reminded of God's redeeming love because the Scripture says that "though your sins are like scarlet, they shall be as white as snow" (Isaiah 1:18). This is a great trigger during the winters here in Cincinnati. Can you imagine the joy that fills me in the midst of a snowstorm? I explode with praise!

The apostle John wrote, "How great is the love the Father has lavished on us, that we should be called children of God! And that is what we are!" (1 John 3:1). When I first read those words, I had to memorize them. Immediately I began to help a dear friend memorize it with me as we traveled on the freeways in Los Angeles. When I added those words, "And this is what we are," I burst out laughing. How good is that? The Father's love has been lavished upon us through his Son and his cross, and by faith we have become children of God.

God loves us, and we are to respond in love. Jesus replied: "'Love the Lord your God with all your heart and with all your soul and with all your mind.' This is the first and greatest commandment. And the second is like it: 'Love your neighbor as yourself'" (Matthew 22:37).

I have come to believe "loving your neighbor" means everyone in our vicinity. This means that we begin with those closest to us, our family—spouse, children, parents, in-laws, etc. No easy task because of their failings and inadequacies, not to mention our own! We are to love those we work with and for, those we worship with and those we meet whether on our street or in the normal routines of life. Remember, biblical love is more than a feeling; it is a choice we make as well as actions that we take.

Loving like God loves means that we don't wait for others to take the first step; after all, God loved us first! Even if our love is not returned, it means that we don't give up. We keep going just as God does with us. And we love our neighbors, whether they deserve it or not—because God's love is gracious, so our love must be gracious as well.

Imagine what a different world this would be if God's people embraced this loving compassion toward our neighbors! The word compassion literally means to "suffer with." This is the kind of love that God wants from us—we care so much, we are committed so much, that even when it is not pleasant, even when others get under our skin, we stay in there, even suffering with those whom God has placed in our vicinity. Of course, by ourselves, this way of living and loving is impossible. That's why in living the Christian life we must always begin and return to the love of God.

Bernard, a great teacher in the church centuries ago, wrote a hymn of God's love:

O hope of every contrite heart;

O joy of all the meek;

To them that fall, how kind Thou art;

How good to those who seek!

But what to those who find? Ah this—

Nor tongue, nor pen can show

The Love of Jesus, what it is.

None but his loved ones know.

God's love is so wonderful that it is hard to put into words. But we try, and we sing. God's love inspires our compassion. Love is where it all starts. Stephen Covey writes that "the main thing is to make the main thing the main thing." (Stephen Covey, First Things First [New York: Simon & Schuster, 1994], p. 75.) Well, God says, love is the main thing. Love is what it is all about. Love is what Jesus wants. This is not breaking news. Ask believers and even nonbelievers what was at the heart of Jesus' message, and many will say, "Love." However, just because Jesus expects us to love does not mean we can do it; and so we pray, "Empower me to love others the way you love me."

REFLECTION QUESTIONS

Chapter 4   Compassion

1. Sharing God's love is one of the greatest privileges of "following Jesus together." Consider a few of those who have been instruments of God's love to you—what specifically do you appreciate about them?

2. One of the ways that I enjoy sharing the love of God is to make phone calls and pray—right over the phone. What are your preferred ways of sharing the love of God? What do think it would be like if you started calling others just to find out how they are and to pray with them?

3. The "towel" and the "ten cow" stories are favorites of mine because they illustrate the touching and transforming power of being loved. How has your experience of the love of God blessed and changed you?

4. Paul not only writes about the love of God, he prays that those he writes to may experience the love of God in Ephesians 3:14-19. Read over that prayer right now and list several ways that praying Paul's prayer could be good for you and those with whom you are praying.

5. Everyone needs a love trigger to heal our damaged receiving mechanism. The birds have been God's "love trigger" for me. What could be a trigger for you and what would keep you from making the decision now?

CHAPTER 5

REPENTANCE

TOUCHED BY THE GRACE AND love of God in prayer, passionate to love God, and inspired to love others the way God loves us, we turn now to face our sin. We ask God: "Wash me clean from every sin."

As disciples of Jesus, we can never be content with sin in our lives. We fall short of God's plan. We still have this old nature within us that is "prone to wander." We find it easier to be selfish than to be unselfish, easier to look out for our own concerns and advancement than to look out for the well-being of our neighbor and the poor.

Jesus is our standard—the measuring stick. When we grasp Jesus' selfless love in his ability to forgive and willingness to sacrifice himself, his spirit and purity of heart in his unself-conscious goodness, we see how far we fall short. Sin becomes obvious and odious when we come into his presence. And so we unashamedly repent and plead to be washed clean from every sin. "If we claim to be without sin, we deceive ourselves and the truth is not in us. If we confess our sins, he is faithful and just and will forgive us our sins and purify us from all unrighteousness" (1 John 1:8-9). I could not live the Christian life without this truth. I memorized 1 John 1:9 the first week I met Christ, in July 1949.

The church is called the Bride of Christ in Revelation 19, and that means we must be concerned with being pure and clean. Imagine a woman walking down the aisle with her wedding dress covered with oil and grease stains, or a groom wearing an elegant white dinner jacket that is dirty and spotted. Everyone would be thinking, "What's the problem? How can this be? Couldn't you get it to the cleaners?" Yes! Get it to the cleaners. We must! That's what even the most careless among us would do. And this is what God has called us to do through confession, repentance, and bringing our "stuff"—everything unworthy of Jesus—to the cross. He is "the perfect cleaners."

Most people find it difficult to believe that God loves them. Almost as many find it difficult, if not impossible, to believe that God forgives them. But he does. King David, the man after God's own heart, had to face the depth of his own sin. Nathan the prophet helped him do that (2 Samuel 12). David could do so because he knew that God is a merciful God.

> Have mercy on me, O God,
>
> according to your unfailing love;
>
> according to your great compassion
>
> blot out my transgressions.
>
> Wash away all my iniquity
>
> and cleanse me from my sin. . . .
>
> Create in me a pure heart, O God,
>
> and renew a steadfast spirit within me. . . .
>
> The sacrifices of God are a broken spirit;
>
> a broken and contrite heart
>
> O God, you will not despise. (Psalm 51:1-2, 10, 17)

This psalm celebrates God's forgiveness as transforming and renewing. More than just being forgiven, when we ask to be "washed clean from every sin," we are asking God to remove the effects of sins we have committed and the sins committed against us. God's forgiveness is creative; it removes the negative and creates something positive. This cleansing is only possible because of Christ's redeeming work on the cross, complete and finished for all eternity. And we must keep in mind that while Christ's saving work is complete, the cleansing begun in this life won't be complete until we step into eternity.

FORGIVING OURSELVES

One of the reasons it is hard to believe that God forgives and cleanses us is that many people cannot forgive themselves. One particular example of this comes to mind for me. I have had many privileges as a pastor, including the opportunity to serve one of the great theologians of our nation. He struggled with a particular sin and came to me with a heavy heart, saying, "I'm hopeless." He had tried to stop his inappropriate behavior on many occasions but could not do so. Over the years, he had failed again and again, and when he came to my home I could see the agony within him.

You might be tempted to think this was a sexual sin of some kind. It wasn't; it was smoking. What grieved him most was a lack of integrity, because he had signed an agreement with the school where he taught that he would not smoke. So not only was he hurting his body, he was hurting his soul through lack of integrity and deceit, and he was limiting his longevity. He was in deep spiritual pain.

I listened to him pour out his heart for some time and finally asked him to read me 1 John 1:9, the passage I referred to at the start of this chapter: "If we confess our sins, he is faithful and just and will forgive us our sins and purify us from all unrighteousness." I listened to him read the passage and then raised the question, "What does this verse mean?" He knew what it meant and had already thought of it many, many times, but he struggled to say so in that moment. Instead, he returned to the level of angst and anguish with which he came into my living room.

This theologian is my friend and a source of real strength for me as a pastor. We know each other well. He was and is a brilliant Bible teacher. So I listened and waited until I believed it to be the proper moment, then I asked him to read 1 John 1:9 again and tell me what it meant. He reluctantly did so and attempted to say that when we confess our sins to God, he will forgive us and wash us clean from all unrighteousness. "But that's for other people, it's not for me. I have repented and failed too many times," he said. His attention was on himself and his repeated failure. He was focusing on how disgusting he found himself, including a significant measure of self-hatred, so he couldn't believe beyond himself. In fact, he came to me because he couldn't believe God's truth was for him. He needed someone else to believe for him. This is true for nearly all of us at some point in our lives.

This time I probably waited five to ten minutes but finally asked him again, "Would you please read me that verse of Scripture one more time and tell me what you think it means?"

I don't remember why or how it happened, but somehow in the midst of reading the verse the third time, his burden lifted. It was evident in his body language. Hope was born when he believed this verse was true and that it was true for him. It meant real forgiveness, real freedom, and a new beginning. His attention moved from the depth of his sin to the wonder and peace of God's forgiveness and mercy. The burden was lifted by God's miracle of grace.

What made the difference? The answer is not complicated. He believed. He believed the Scripture was true and that it was true for him. He knew all along that God forgives sinners when they repent. He had shared that with hundreds and maybe thousands of people. Now he believed that it applied to him and that he was forgiven and washed clean from all unrighteousness. He left my home a new person. He has been used powerfully by God to bring God's grace to others.

I want to shout this from the rooftop. Everyone needs to hear this. Jesus is not surprised by your sin. He will never say, "Oops! That is a sin I did not foresee—that is a sin I did not die for." It is right that we take our sin seriously. But when we take our sin so seriously that we believe God will not and cannot forgive us, we dishonor our Lord because he has paid the ultimate price of suffering and dying on the cross, which was necessary for our full forgiveness and redemption. And he is most blessed when we receive his forgiveness and celebrate his grace. He is not blessed when we continue to live under the burden of our guilt and shame that he has already taken upon himself.

"Wash me clean from every sin" is a daily request, because receiving forgiveness and forgiving ourselves is hard and our need is constant. This reminds me of one day when I received a phone call from a young pastor in the West whom I had known for many years. He was a deeply dedicated Christian and an effective pastor for whom I had great respect and affection. He had been used powerfully in the lives of many young people and had unusual gifts of compassion, teaching, and follow-through. He said to me, "Jerry, I need to see you. It is urgent. Is there any way you could take time to meet me soon?" He was only in town for a few days. I told him I was traveling from Cincinnati to Indianapolis over the weekend to speak to around a thousand men about sexual purity.

If he were able to travel with me, we could talk for two hours each way. He was available, and so we went together.

On the first leg of the trip he poured out his heart. He had gone on a ministry trip to the South during which he became sexually involved with a young married woman on the team. He knew it was wrong. He had confessed this to his wife and then, with the young woman, to her husband. The disappointment and anger of both spouses was inevitable. His sense of remorse and failure had neutralized his life and ministry for nearly two years. He had no sense of forgiveness from God, and he could not forgive himself. He had lost his passion for ministry and was locked in despair. He knew this happened to some people, but he could not believe it had happened to him. He presumed he had forfeited any possibility of leading or blessing God's people.

That's where we were when we arrived for my meeting in Indianapolis. We were greatly blessed by the men gathered there and the quality of worship and teaching. When we got back in the car to come home, I summarized our conversation on the way to Indianapolis and then asked him several questions: Do you think God was surprised by your sin? Do you believe that Christ died for that sin or only for your other sins? Is that sin too big for God's grace to overcome in order to use you again in the lives of his people?

As we traveled back to Cincinnati I told him that I was deeply disappointed. He believed he deserved to be broken by his sin and that he needed to struggle. He was right. We dare not take any sin lightly, but this sin is especially serious because of what it does to us and our family relationships and the family of God. It violates the integrity of both marriages and is a sin that is incredibly prevalent in American culture. Our culture does not support fidelity within marriage; it is absolutely essential that God's people do so.

I said to him, "Do you want to know what makes me angry? It is not your sin of adultery, although I hate what that has done. It has been devastating to your wife and the woman's family; that is heartbreaking. But what makes me most angry is that for two years you have allowed that sin, that betrayal of your wife and the congregation, to neutralize your walk with God, your experience and celebration of God's grace and mercy and your freedom in Christ. The devil has had a field day in your life, keeping you from being able to get beyond yourself and your sin so that you could lift your people to the Lord, who are struggling with their own sins. For two years you have not been able to bring God's grace to them for their sins, which they have desperately needed from you.

"I do not, for one moment, minimize the depth of your sin. It is a horrendous transgression because of the way it has wounded the honor of God, two marriages and families, and a beloved congregation. But that is why Jesus died. He does not love you any less. He has paid the price for your forgiveness, and instead of running into his arms pleading for mercy and asking to be washed clean, you have allowed that sin to undermine and rob you of your fruitful ministry for two years. Why did you wait two years to come seeking help that could lift you into the merciful arms of our Lord?"

I am glad to tell you that he has experienced God's grace again and knows that he has been washed clean from every sin. God is using him powerfully among his people. And that can be true for you, too, if you are struggling with some hidden sin. Don't let it remain hidden. Share it with someone who can help you bring it to the Lord so that he can wash you clean. Jesus welcomed the prodigal home. He welcomes you. There is a towel on every limb.

THE DEPTHS OF SIN

This washing from sin must go deep, all the way down to the depths of our hearts, because that is where sin resides. Jesus said,

> What comes out of a person is what defiles them. For it is from within, out of a person's heart, that evil thoughts come— sexual immorality, theft, murder, adultery, greed, malice, deceit, lewdness, envy, slander, arrogance and folly. All these evils come from inside and defile a person. (Mark 7:20-23)

The seven deadly sins are the historic and classic catalogue of the sins of the heart: pride, envy, greed, gluttony, lust, anger, and sloth. They are deadly because they destroy our souls and our relationships. I have my own version of the deadly sins: self-righteousness/pride, lust, broken/unforgiving relationships, and a lack of respect and awe for God. I list these sins because they are the ones that I am most aware of within me. These are the sins that I see we tend to wink at—they are so common, so pervasive, and sometimes presumed as inevitable. No! They are not inevitable, and they are not invisible. So you and I must confront them. "Wash me clean from every sin" is not merely a prayer for forgiveness! It is a prayer for changing the way we live.

SELF-RIGHTEOUSNESS AND PRIDE

Jesus confronted self-righteousness again and again. In the parable of the Pharisee and the tax collector (Luke 18:9-14), Jesus tells a story that expressed his disdain for self-righteousness. Two people are described as going into the temple to pray at the same time. First Jesus relates the prayer of the Pharisee, who said, "God, I thank you that I am not like other people—robbers, evildoers, adulterers—or even like this tax collector. I fast twice a week and give a tenth of all I get." Then Jesus describes the tax collector: "He would not even look up to heaven, but beat his breast and said, 'God, have mercy on me, a sinner.'" Then Jesus makes his point: "I tell you that this man, rather than the other, went home justified before God. For all those who exalt themselves will be humbled, and those who humble themselves will be exalted."

The danger we face when we follow Jesus as Lord in a more passionate and disciplined way is that the Evil One draws our attention to the fact: "Hey, I'm really making progress!" I am sobered by the message of the senior tempter Screwtape to his protégé Wormwood that C. S. Lewis provides in his book *The Screwtape Letters*:

Your patient has become humble; have you drawn his attention to the fact? All virtues are less formidable to us once the man is aware that he has them, but this is specially true of humility. Catch him at the moment when he is really poor in spirit and smuggle into his mind the gratifying reflection, "By Jove! I'm being humble," and almost immediately pride—

pride at his own humility—will appear.[12]

Before we know it, and with the best intentions, our pursuit of humility or any other Christian virtue can become a source of pride and self-righteousness. Jesus dealt with self-righteousness and pride more seriously than almost any sin. Both refocus our attention on ourselves. They weaken our faith and undermine our capacity to love our Lord and to love each other.

I must face this directly. Since I come from a family of high achievement, pride is a continual temptation for me. I remind myself constantly that God will not tolerate pride or self-righteousness. James the brother of our Lord put it this way: "God opposes the proud but gives grace to the humble" (James 4:6). James understood this because he personally saw genuine humility in the life of Jesus.

Peter too saw humility in the life and example of Jesus. While the Gospels portray Peter as brash and self-confident, his experience with Jesus changed him. In his first letter to the leaders of young churches of the Roman world, rather than describing himself as a great apostle, he writes to fellow elders (1 Peter 5:1) and says:

> In the same way, you who are younger, submit yourselves to your elders. All of you clothe yourselves with humility toward one another, because, "God opposes the proud but shows favor to the humble and oppressed."

> Humble yourselves, therefore, under God's mighty hand, that he may lift you up in due time. (1 Peter 5:5-6)

---

12 (C. S. Lewis, *Screwtape Letters*, Signature Classics [San Francisco: HarperSanFrancisco, 2002], p. 153).

Self-centeredness is one of the more obvious manifestations of pride. In the first chapter of *The Purpose Driven Life* Rick Warren writes, "It's not about you"[13] This statement confronts our most basic sin. We place ourselves and our concerns in the center of the universe. We think that life is "about me." Francis Chan, in his book *Crazy Love*[14], exposes the foolishness of such thinking. He invites us to consider ourselves as one of five hundred extras in an upcoming movie in which we end up being on screen for only two-fifths of a second. After the movie is released, we rent a theater and invite our friends to come see that movie and tell them that it is all about us. After seeing the movie our friends rightly think us foolish and self-centered.

Chan then invites us to consider God's story in the Bible—creation and fall; God's call to Abraham, Isaac, and Jacob; the story of Joseph; the nation of Israel as slaves in Egypt delivered to the Promised Land through Moses; the rise of the judges, kings, and prophets—all leading to Jesus, his birth, death, resurrection, and ascension. Then of course there are the twenty centuries of church growth and the two billion people today who follow him. The story of the Bible is God's story about God's kingdom, not ours. In light of God's story, relatively speaking, we have our two-fifths of a second on earth. When put in these terms, we can see how ridiculous it is to be self-centered and think that the story is about us.

When I read those two pages in *Crazy Love*, I burst out laughing with my wife. I was laughing because of the audacity of anyone believing that the story is about them—and then having to acknowledge to myself, and my wife that, more often than not, I have thought the

---

13 (Rick Warren, *The Purpose Driven Life* [Grand Rapids: Zondervan, 2002], p. 17).
14 (Colorado Springs: David C. Cook, 2013, pp. 44-45)

story was about me! The danger in admitting such a thought now is the presumption of thinking that by doing so I have now faced up to the utter foolishness of thinking that way and of thinking that I have now gotten over it for good.

There is a reason why Jesus said, "Whoever wants to be my disciple must deny themselves and take up their cross daily and follow me" (Luke 9:23). He is not calling us to just a little self-denial—perhaps giving up desserts or whatever our favorite pleasure might be. He is calling us to the denial of self and the impulse to build our lives, our families, and our endeavors around our own interests. We must not think that way. It is not about me. It's not about you. We must get over it. "Lord, wash me clean from every sin."

LUST

Along with pride and selfishness, lust is burning within our hearts. It has always been there, of course, but our modern world has gone crazy over illicit portrayals of nudity and a variety of sex acts. God has given us a wonderful gift in our sexuality, and we have taken that which is good, beautiful, and life-giving and made it cheap and self-serving. What was intended to enrich and nourish enduring relationships within marriage has become a means of producing shallow, throwaway relationships. Confronted by the barrage of Hollywood and the media, we must remember that God has given us the gift of sexual intimacy to deepen the love between a man and a woman within the bonds of marriage. God's intention for our sexuality was to be a means of nurturing marital love and as well as conceiving children and rearing them in an atmosphere of mutual appreciation and trust.

I have given my life for twenty-five years to fighting against this desecration of sexuality. But this doesn't mean that I am immune from it. I need to guard my heart and mind like everyone else, and this determines what I allow myself to watch and what movies I will attend. I have given up watching *Dancing with the Stars* because it produces in me strong and inappropriate thoughts that linger. It wasn't the dancing that attracted me.

Lust is easily produced and by it we are sexually seduced. It can only be limited and channeled into wholesome, healthy, and growing relationships within marriage through strong faith, focused discipline, accountability, and widespread social support. Since that helpful and necessary support from the broader culture is gone, how will we get the genie back in the bottle? Only by surrendering to Christ as Lord and mutual accountability with other growing believers. We cry out, "Lord, wash me clean from every sin." Sexual purity is even more of a challenge in the age of the internet. We need him to strengthen our intentions for purity and help us use filtering and accountability devices.

BROKEN/UNFORGIVING RELATIONSHIPS

Jesus is all about relationships, and he is all about forgiveness. The two go hand-in-hand in a world in which we sin against God and against one another. The only way that God can keep a healthy relationship with us is by means of forgiveness, and the only way that we can keep healthy relationships with each other is through the same means.

Jesus came to forgive. He died to forgive. He forgave from the cross, and he commands us to forgive today. Jesus is all about love, self-giving love. He calls us to love our enemies. He is the great Healer and Reconciler. In our Lord's Prayer he prayed, "Forgive us our debts as we forgive our debtors." And then, right after giving the prayer to his disciples, Jesus immediately emphasized the portion on forgiveness: "For if you forgive other people when they sin against you, your heavenly Father will also forgive you" (Matthew 6:14). How could any Christian miss the priority of this truth in the mind of Jesus? Reconciled relationships are essential for Jesus and for those who resolve to follow him.

Jesus addresses forgiveness and relationships on another occasion when he was instructing his disciples. He tells the parable of the unforgiving servant, in which a servant who owed an impossible debt was completely forgiven and then turned around and refused to forgive someone who owed him a very small sum. "Then the master called the servant in. 'You wicked servant,' he said. 'I canceled all that debt of yours because you begged me to. Shouldn't you have had mercy on your fellow servant just as I had on you?' In anger his master turned him over to the jailers to be tortured, until he should pay back all he owed." Then Jesus said, "This is how my heavenly Father will treat each of you unless you forgive your brother or sister from your heart" (Matthew 18:32-35). This may seem harsh to some. But Jesus wants us to know the truth because he knows the truth will set us free (John 8:32). And that is his deepest desire for each of us.

Jesus' priority is restoring relationships. Relationships are broken when there is no forgiveness, and relationships are restored when forgiveness is given. We see this so clearly in the parable of the prodigal son, when the father eagerly received his wayward son back into the family. I have a friend whose guiding rule during a time when his sons were experimenting with drugs and promiscuity was "keep the relationship." Instead of cutting them off, he and his wife kept contact with them and kept forgiving them even though they were grieved and disappointed by their children's behavior. Eventually their constant contact provided a bridge back into health, godly behavior, and the restoration of the family.

It is a harsh reality that broken relationships are so frequently tolerated within families—even Christian families. Why is this so? And broken relationships are tolerated within churches and within and between denominations. Probably the most widespread sin in our world is shallow love toward God and one another within the body of Christ and beyond. God's love is a forgiving love that keeps the relationship even at the cost of the death of his Son. This is another way in which we are called to deny ourselves, take up our cross daily, and follow Jesus. Real forgiveness is impossible apart from God's grace, and so we must pray, "Lord, wash me clean from every sin."

SHALLOW WORSHIP

The last sin I want to address is shallow worship. I have struggled with rushing into the presence of God throughout my Christian life. And often while in God's presence I have struggled to stay focused and be attentive. I wish this were not true; I wish I didn't need to share this with you. But I believe that apart from transparency and vulnerability, this book would lose its integrity and blessing.

My focus for many years has been enjoying fellowship with God— God's love for me and my love for God. I believe in the majesty, greatness, and glory of God, his awesome and supreme power. And yet, looking at my devotional patterns over the years, I can see they were often distracted and shallow. I am especially aware of this when I contrast my personal preparation I have made for meeting with God with preparation I have made to meet with great leaders. I have had meetings with Ronald Reagan, George H. W. Bush, Pope John Paul II, Billy Graham, Bill Bright, Paul Rader (the retired world-wide General of the Salvation Army), and even a telephone conversation with Mother Teresa. I prepared my mind and heart carefully and thoroughly for each meeting and had a sense of awe and respect as I met them. However, great as they are, they are only human. They are and were only leaders among some of the people in the world, all of whom were created by our great God.

In light of God's glory and greatness, how is it possible that I would not prepare with much greater care to enter God's presence? How could my mind wander in the midst of prayer? How could my attention drift so easily from God onto me and my needs? Or on the needs of others?

In the Old Testament, Jewish believers would not even speak or write the name of God. And only one person would enter into the Holy of Holies each year. In the next line of the Prayer Covenant we will further explore our need to worship as a way of life. But before we get to that request, we need to acknowledge that our worship is shallow and falls short of giving God the glory he deserves and demands.

THE SIN OFFENSIVE

Until Jesus comes back, we will wrestle with sin. In your battle, keep short accounts with God. Every time you become aware of a sinful motivation, thought, or action, confess immediately and repent quickly. Right away! Martin Luther wrote that he couldn't keep birds from flying over his head, and he could not keep sinful thoughts from flashing through his mind. But while he could not keep the birds from flying over his head, he could keep them from building nests in his hair. In the same way, he could keep sin from building a home in his heart. Don't let sin build a home in your heart. Don't let yourself think sinful thoughts and relish them. The way I deal with those thoughts is to immediately say the name of Jesus over and over and ask him to fill my mind with himself and his truth. Then I seek to quote Scripture. Keep on the offensive against sin by filling your mind with the Lord, Scripture, and godly thoughts. The apostle Paul wrote, "Whatever is true, whatever is noble, whatever is right, whatever is pure, whatever is lovely, whatever is admirable—if anything is excellent or praiseworthy—think about such things" (Philippians 4:8).

Furthermore, stay close to other growing Christians. This is essential. I have found having an accountability partner to be a great help in the battle with sin—in fact, I have two of them! We talk regularly about the state of our hearts. We have given permission to ask each other hard and searching questions that force us to look deep into our hearts so that we keep short accounts with God and each other.

The gift of God's forgiveness is wonderful. David wrote:

Blessed are those

whose transgressions are forgiven,

whose sins are covered.

Blessed are those

whose sin the Lord does not count against them

and in whose spirit there is no deceit (Psalm 32:1-2).

And so we pray, "Lord, wash me clean from every sin."

REFLECTION QUESTIONS

Chapter 5   Repentance

1. "Wash me clean from every sin"—how does this sentence help you understand what happens when we repent and God forgives?

2. One of the reasons we find it difficult to receive God's forgiveness is because it is hard to forgive ourselves. How do you respond when your past sins and moral failures come to mind? What steps can you take to locate someone with whom you can bring your sins to the Lord?

3. Asking God to "wash me clean from every sin" is not only a prayer for healing the effects of sins we have personally committed, but of healing the effects of sins committed against us. In what ways might this dimension of spiritual cleansing impact your life?

4. Asking God to "wash me clean" is not only a prayer about sins we have committed, it is also a prayer for deliverance from committing sin. Of the sins I refer to (self-righteousness

and pride, lust, broken/unforgiving relationships, and shallow worship), which do you struggle with and what are you going to do about them?

5. Having an accountability partner or two can be a great help in living a godly life. Keep in mind that it is also a challenge, as we must seek to be transparent and vulnerable with our partner. Who can be an accountability partner for you? When and how are you going to approach them?

WORSHIP

IN THE CHAPTER ON COMPASSION, I wrote about love and the birds—birds are the trigger that reminds me that God loves me. More people talk to me about "the birds" than anything else I have ever said. It's so practical. The birds are everywhere, and the constant and repeated sight of them is a constant and repeated reminder of God's love. Not only do birds remind me of God's love, but they also inspire me to worship. When I remember that God loves me, my heart overflows. Without question, because of the birds, I worship repeatedly many times a day, almost every day.

When I think about it, more than just the birds, there are constant inspirations to worship all around me. All creation inspires me to worship—the ocean every year when my extended family gathers on the shore of North Carolina; the mountains in Colorado where Patty and I spend summers; and the stars on a warm night, as the mountains are covered at dusk and the stars begin to shine from the vast expanse of the sky, which stretches out beyond imagining. Whether standing on the shore at night or outside in the mountains, Psalm 19:1 often comes to mind: "The heavens declare the glory of God; the skies proclaim the work of his hands."

This chapter is about worship. The Prayer Covenant begins with gratitude for God's grace and love, then progresses on to love for God, which then directs our love to others. Love then also leads us into repentance and a heartfelt request for forgiveness. Now the Prayer Covenant makes a strong request of God: that he would enable us to give him the praise, glory, and adoration he deserves. "Enable me to praise you, O Lord, with all my heart."

This line of the prayer comes from Psalm 9:1: "I will praise you, O LORD, with all my heart; I will tell of all your wonderful deeds."

We can't truly know God without responding in worship. What is worship? It is praise. It is acknowledging the value and worth of God. What we must get clearly in mind is that anything less than focused, wholehearted worship is unworthy of our mighty God. We want him to be known, loved, honored, revered, exalted, glorified, and obeyed. Linger over this line when you pray the Prayer Covenant. Ask God to enable you to worship, and then fill your heart with praise.

While worship is my desire and my joy, we still work at worship—it is a holy work worthy of everything we have to give. To praise and worship God is to get outside ourselves and enter into proper relationship with our God as the great God. I want to use all the resources and pathways available to me to enter into worship. I have found that Scripture inspires me to worship, dear friends with whom I have followed Jesus inspire me to worship, the church inspires me to worship, and my family inspires me to worship. Above all, the character of God—the majesty and holiness of God—inspires me to worship.

SCRIPTURE AND WORSHIP

When I think about how I have experienced the joy of worship, the Scriptures come to mind as the source and foundation from which I start. I have had three "life verses" (really each is a few verses) during my fifty-six-plus years of ministry. The first focused on the Holy Spirit providing "rivers of living water," drawn from John 7:37-39. The second focused on my desire to sanctify myself for the well-being of those I love, drawn from John 17:17-19. The third, which I believe is the one I'll dwell on for the remainder of my life, focuses on worship and ending well. It is Psalm 146:1-2: "Praise the LORD. Praise the LORD, O my soul. I will praise the Lord all my life: I will sing praise to my God as long as I live."

While I have chosen specific "life verses," there are many verses that inspire me to worship. One that I especially love comes from Lamentations. I have memorized it in the Revised Standard Version and share it with you from that version.

But this I call to mind,

and therefore I have hope:

The steadfast love of the LORD never ceases,

his mercies never come to an end;

they are new every morning;

great is thy faithfulness.

"The LORD is my portion," says my soul,

"therefore I will hope in him"

(Lamentations 3:21-24 RSV).

When I think about verses of Scripture that inspire me, the "plums" that I come back to again and again come from the Psalms:

Shout for joy to God, all the earth!

Sing the glory of his name;

make his praise glorious.

Say to God, "How awesome are your deeds!"

(Psalm 66:1-3)

I will extol the LORD at all times;

his praise will always be on my lips.

I will glory in the LORD;

let the afflicted hear and rejoice.

Glorify the LORD with me;

let us exalt his name together.

(Psalm 34:1-3)

I will sing of the LORD's great love forever;

with my mouth I will make your faithfulness known

through all generations.

I will declare that your love stands firm forever,

that you have established your faithfulness in heaven itself.

(Psalm 89 1-2)

The other section of Scripture I turn to most frequently for worship is the book of Revelation. I love the vision John describes in which God is on his throne surrounded by innumerable heavenly and earthly creatures singing and praising, in Revelation 4 and 5.

Day and night they never stop saying:

"Holy, holy, holy

is the Lord God Almighty,'

who was, and is, and is to come."

(Revelation 4:8)

Then I looked and heard the voice of many angels, numbering thousands upon thousands, and ten thousand times ten thousand. They encircled the throne and the living creatures and the elders. In a loud voice they were saying:

"Worthy is the Lamb, who was slain,

> to receive power and wealth and wisdom and strength
>
> and honor and glory and praise!"
>
> Then I heard every creature in heaven and on earth and under the earth and on the sea, and all that is in them, saying:
>
> "To him who sits on the throne and to the Lamb
>
> be praise and honor and glory and power,
>
> for ever and ever!"
>
> The four living creatures said, "Amen," and the elders fell down and worshiped.
>
> (Revelation 5:11-14)

I have memorized these verses that I have shared with you, along with many others. I go through them systematically during my devotional times each day. As I recall and rehearse those I have memorized, it seems that one or two each day speak directly to me and draw me into worship. There are a variety of outstanding devotionals available that have a verse or two of Scripture with supporting commentary. I find Oswald Chambers's *My Utmost for His Highest* an outstanding resource. However, the best resource for worship, pure and simple, is the Word of God. Get into the Scriptures daily. Read a chapter a day, read several verses a day, find a Scripture reading plan, use a Bible study guide—whatever you do and however you do it, get into the Scriptures daily and let the Scriptures get into you.

PEOPLE

I have repeatedly been inspired to worship by dear friends with whom I have been privileged to pursue the Lord. As a new believer the first half of my second summer at Young Life Camp, I was on work crew with Charlie Normant. We got up each morning to meet the Lord, and as we did, we got closer to the Lord and to each other. That following winter after camp we kept in touch, writing frequently. This was during the time of the Korean conflict. Charlie joined the Marines and went to the front. Later I got word that he died. I received two letters from him that he must have mailed just before he was killed. Can you imagine what it was like to read them? Because of our spiritual friendship, I felt responsible and inspired to keep going and keep growing in the Lord, in ways that I have never gotten over.

Who are your spiritual friends and companions? If you stop to think about it, perhaps as you look back on your life, you will discover that your spiritual growth has come, in large measure, because others have cared for you, prayed for you, prayed with you, and invested in you. Thank God for those people. Pray for them and pursue God with them. The Prayer Covenant is all about "following Jesus together," and God intends us to grow with and through them. It is so rich to pray, praise, and worship with those who are walking beside you. The apostle Paul wrote to his friends who comprised the church of Philippi: "I thank my God every time I remember you. In all my prayers for all of you, I always pray with joy because of your partnership in the gospel from the first day until now, being confident of this, that he who began a good work in you will carry it on to completion until the day of Christ Jesus" (Philippians 1:3-6).

THE CHURCH

We can't think about spiritual friends and companions for very long without thinking about the church. When I came back from Young Life camp, I joined the Queen Anne United Presbyterian Church in Seattle. They continued to nourish me; the pastor, Cliff Smith, took a special interest in me and was responsible for encouraging me to pursue my theological studies and first years of ministry in Pittsburgh.

I love to worship God alone daily on my porch, in my study, or in other spaces that have become holy meeting places. But I also need the gathering of God's people in Sunday worship services. When I am surrounded with those who are worshiping, I am encouraged and lifted into worship. It's like logs thrown into a burning fire— when the fire is low or flickering, the new log may not catch. When the fire is blazing, the fresh log will burn too. When those around me adore God, it strikes a spark in my heart.

There are a rich variety of ways to worship the Lord with others. I know about a Bible study that does more than just study the Bible. Before the members begin to look at the Scripture, they spend at least ten minutes in quiet worship—they don't intercede for their prayer concerns until they have been before the Lord in silence, and they are not Quakers! The leader of the study believes that most of us are far too busy outwardly and inwardly—and all the busyness keeps us from connecting intimately with God. The silence allows them to slow down and pay attention to God. That amount of silence would make most people I know very uncomfortable, but not them. They bring their hearts before the Lord and listen for the tender whispers of the Spirit. You can sense the rich depth of worship that fills the room. There is something powerful about a shared worshipful silence. There is such a thing as an empty silence, and then there is a full silence. Their silence is very full.

One of the most memorable times of worship I have had was an experience of quiet. I recall a time when I had recently come to College Hill Church and met with Buzz Richter, who was also on staff. We decided to conclude our meeting in prayer. We began our prayer with a few moments of quiet, and then the quiet just grew; five minutes to ten minutes, and then more. We were quiet for about half an hour—my sense of the presence of God was so strong that I couldn't lead out audibly. Words seemed like an intrusion into that full presence of God, who filled the room. When I think back on that experience I am reminded of Psalm 46:10, "Be still and know that I am God."

I have attended many churches and experienced worship in a variety of ways. I have worshiped in congregations that are traditional and contemporary. I have worshiped in churches where the choir was tremendous and where the choir was not so good.

I have found that it is not the quality or the style of music that most inspires me to worship, although that is helpful. What most inspires me is the worship of the worship leader and the choir members themselves. They didn't just perform; they led in worship. What makes the difference is whether the choir director is passionate for worship. This is not just a gifting, talent, or skill; the Spirit inspires it.

In the assembly of God's people for worship, music has such an important role. I love to sing traditional hymns such as "Be Thou My Vision," "Great Is Thy Faithfulness" or "When I Survey the Wondrous Cross." Of course I love to worship with choruses/

worship songs such as "As a Deer Pants," "I Love You Lord," or "In This Very Room." Some people like only one style of worship, and some churches conduct worship services that are targeted to these different preferences. Some people like just the organ; others want guitar, keyboard, and drums. My son Stephen is a pastor and told me just last week that he sometimes feels like he is pastoring three congregations in one church because so many people gather around the different types of music. I love all the styles of music and worship! At College Hill, we developed blended worship services that incorporated both traditional and contemporary music. For me, it is not so much the style of music as whether those leading are really worshiping or just performing.

Come to think of it, worship goes far beyond music. We might be inclined to think that it is really preaching, or the preacher, or the room where we worship, or some other element. But worship is so much more than the sum of what we do or say or any one element. Worship is a spiritual gift. It is more than music; more than preaching; more than emotion; more than our minds; more than our actions. This of course is why we must pray "Enable me to praise you, O Lord, with all my heart."

FAMILY WORSHIP

Family worship has had a profound impact on me and my family. Worship, from the beginning, was foundational for us. When I fell in love with Patty, I wanted to worship with her. When we had kids, I wanted to worship with them. I am sure that my passion for worship would have driven my kids bananas without intervention. I was a case! Patty tempered and guided me. She told me, "When you play with the kids more, we will pray with the kids more."

It was common to worship as a family after dinner for about a half an hour on a regular basis. Not every day, but frequently and regularly. Before we got up to clean up and do the dishes, we would read Scripture, sing songs, and share. Our children were shaped into worshipers and leaders as they first participated in and then led in worship.

Family vacations were a great time for worship as we drove in the car. The first thing I wanted to do when we got in the car was sing. And as we traveled we would start every day with worship. It was so natural for me to worship. But I know I can be intense. I am so thankful for Patty's ability to keep me in balance so that my intensity didn't drive the children away from the Lord.

That tradition has carried on from our children to our grandchildren and great-grandchildren. On every day but Wednesday, we spend an hour in worship when the extended family gets together each year with our children and their spouses, our grandchildren and their spouses and great grandchildren. Our grandchildren have been leading the opening worship music for the past fifteen years with adults doing the teaching. It is this worship time, and Patty's cooking, that I believe our grandchildren will remember most about our family.

For much of our family experience we had an extended family, with young Christians who wanted to follow the Lord, living with us. Eventually there were over forty people who were part of our family for six months to three years. Some of them brought the gift of worship and strengthened our singing and sharing. David Tedford brought the gift of fun into our family. I love fun, but fun was not natural for me. David helped us in so many ways, even helping us cope with young tempers that would flare in unhealthy ways. Every person who lived with us brought gifts that enriched our family and family worship, and their presence blessed us all.

WORSHIPING THE HOLY GOD

Worship takes us into the depths and heights when we approach God as holy. The Lord's Prayer sets the tone: "Our Father in heaven, holy is your name." We live in a culture where people use the name of God flippantly, repeatedly, and casually, especially in films and on TV. People misuse the name without any sense of shame, because we are desensitized to the sacredness and majesty of God. So we need help to do what should be natural and right, the heartfelt, holy worship of God.

This sense of holiness is exactly how Jesus teaches us to pray: "Our Father in heaven, hallowed be your name" (Matthew 6:9). This is the starting place of prayer.

Wholehearted worship and the holiness of God are bound up together. We get a glimpse of this when the door of heaven is opened to the apostle John in the book of Revelation. What he sees in heaven is what we all will do one day—worship God, completely and regularly: "Day and night they never stop saying, 'Holy, holy, holy is the Lord God Almighty, who was, and is, and is to come'" (Revelation 4:8).

God is holy, and he is to be worshiped—this is about awe, respect, and adoration. The very first action required of Moses by God in the burning bush encounter was that he must take his sandals off because he was "standing on holy ground" (Exodus 3:5). That meeting with God as the holy God, for Moses and for all of us, was a life-changing experience. R. C. Sproul, in his book *The Holiness of God*, wrote of his awakening to God. Literally summoned from his bed in the middle of the night as a college student,

> [I] walked across campus to the chapel and entered.
>
> An icy chill started at the base of my spine and crept up my neck. Fear swept over me. I fought the impulse to run from the foreboding presence that gripped me.
>
> The terror passed, soon followed by another wave. This wave was different. It flooded my soul with unspeakable peace, a peace that brought instant rest and repose to my troubled spirit. At once I wanted to linger there. To say nothing. To do nothing. Simply to bask in the presence of God.
>
> That moment was life transforming. Something deep in my spirit was being settled once for all. From this moment there could be no turning back; there could be no erasure of the indelible imprint of its power. I was alone with God. A holy God. An awesome God. A God who could fill me with terror in one second and fill me with peace the next. I knew in that hour that I had tasted of the Holy Grail. Within me was born a new thirst that could never be fully satisfied in this world. I resolved to learn more, to pursue this God who lived in dark Gothic cathedrals and who invaded my dormitory room to rouse me from complacent slumber.[15]

God is worthy to be worshiped, so "let us be thankful, and so worship God acceptably with reverence and awe for our God is a consuming fire" (Hebrews 12:28).

---

15 (R. C. Sproul, The Holiness of God [Carol Stream, IL: Tyndale House Publishers, 1985], pp. 3-5).

THE WORK OF WORSHIP

I wrote in the last chapter that one of the sins I continually have to repent of is rushing into the presence of the holy God without adequate preparation, and then allowing myself to be distracted when I do pray. But I work at worshiping God better. I have been working at worshiping God since I first became a Christian.

The day after I met Christ in Colorado at the Young Life camp, Mike McCutchen invited me to join him the next morning at 6:30 a.m. to meet with Jesus. He told me, "Jerry, now you know Christ. Christians spend time with Jesus at the beginning of each day." Since Mike was a more mature Christian and a star basketball player in Seattle whom I highly respected, I wanted to spend time with him. So the next day he got me started on a daily worship practice. He taught me that we could spend time with Jesus every day. Wow! Don't pass over that sentence lightly. What a gift that was to me as a new Christian. For some time I assumed all Christians did that and only discovered later that lots of Christians were casual or even unconcerned with a daily devotional time. So the discipline of time alone with God began with me from the first day of my life with Christ. I have followed his example over eighty percent of my days for sixty-plus years. Thank you, Mike. That has been one of the greatest gifts I ever received.

We need to work at worship—but not because it is drudgery. On the contrary, it is a joy and a delight. But worship calls us beyond ourselves, and this is not easy. Remember, it is not about you! We must lift our eyes from ourselves to him. We need to worship God with others on Sunday morning and then worship regularly throughout the week. Mother Teresa was once asked what was necessary to live a godly life. She replied, "Spend an hour a day in prayer and never do anything you know to be wrong." Many people call this regular act of worship a quiet time, while others call it devotions. Whatever you call it, the point is to be with Jesus regularly in quiet, precious, and intimate ways.

Jesus used his time in Mary and Martha's home to teach this pivotal truth. Mary sat at Jesus' feet to be taught. She was attentive to Jesus, while Martha was busy doing things. Martha was preparing the meal and was frustrated with Mary for her lack of helping.

> She came to him and asked, "Lord, don't you care that my sister has left me to do the work by myself? Tell her to help me!"
>
> "Martha, Martha," the Lord answered, "you are worried and upset about many things, but only one thing is needed. Mary has chosen what is better, and it will not be taken away from her." (Luke 10:40-42)

Only one thing in that situation was needed. It was the "with me" principle. The only thing needful is that we be with Jesus often enough that he can make the adventure all he intends it to be. What a privilege it is to spend unhurried time each morning with the sovereign Lord of the universe. Who would choose to miss that divine appointment?

Moses knew the importance of the "with me" principle. He worked at worship, too. As he led the nation, he set up a tent on the outskirts of the Israelite camp, called the tent of meeting, so that people could inquire of the Lord. It was in that tent that Moses himself had the regular experience of meeting with God "face to face" (Exodus 33:11). When we have a quiet time with God, we are establishing a tent of meeting. We create a place outside the busy routines of our lives to be with God.

We need quiet times because we need to worship God. He is the one who makes sense of life, not just for times of crisis but for the task of living. In a quiet time I am able to see into the spiritual depths of reality in which God is present. In a quiet time I can look not only at God but also at myself. God is always meeting us, always caring for us, and always directing us, but it is possible to be blind to his presence. Perhaps you have never experienced his presence in the first place. But you can.

Those who know God best seek God most, as A. W. Tozer affirms.

> Come near to the holy men and women of the past and you will soon feel the heat of their desire after God. They mourned for Him, they prayed and wrestled and sought for Him day and night, in season and out, and when they had found Him the finding was all the sweeter for the long seeking.[16]

Cultivate this inner fire of God's holiness by worshiping him. Seize times to be alone with God, in special "set aside" places, so that it gets you out of the rush of life. Maybe you have a special room in your house or a special chair you sit in. Maybe you have a place on your back patio. Maybe it is your living room after you have turned off the television. Go where you need to go and do what you need to do to be alone with God. Pursue the heart-satisfying presence of God. When you go to church on Sundays, don't be just an attender. Go to worship; be a worshiper. Don't go looking just to "get something out of the sermon." Don't be halfhearted. From the depths of your being, go there to give God glory. And as you go about your daily activities, at work and at home, let wholehearted worship of God be your motivation.

---

16 (A. W. Tozer, The Pursuit of God [Camp Hill, PA: WingSpread Publishers, 1993], p. 15)

CONCLUSION

Worship is a gift. Worship is a joy. Worship is what we do now and what we will do in eternity. Worship can emerge spontaneously throughout each day. Worship is what you do with others on Sunday morning, what you do by yourself in your daily quiet time, what you do when you meet with your spiritual friends, and what you can do with your family around the dinner table after a meal. Worship can be what you do when you see the birds, look at the stars, or stand on the shore as you feel the wind on your face and hear the crash of the waves. God is the source of it all. Worship him. There is no greater privilege.

It is possible that you have known the joy of worship, but then somehow it slipped away. As Israel was about to enter the Promised Land, Moses warned them: "Only be careful, and watch yourselves closely so that you do not forget the things your eyes have seen or let them slip from your heart as long as you live" (Deuteronomy 4:9). If you need to, start again right now. Desire to be with and adore our holy, majestic God. Worship is what fuels our hearts as we pray: "Enable me to praise you, O Lord, with all my heart."

REFLECTION QUESTIONS

Chapter 6   Worship

1. The birds have been essential worship triggers for me. What are the "triggers" that remind and inspire you to worship?

2. The Scriptures are foundational for worshiping God. Which verses do you find most helpful?

3. Who are your spiritual companions with whom you share the joy of worshiping God? Who else can you add, and what are you going to do to connect with them? What role does a church have in your worship of God?

4. Our family worship has been essential, and has borne wonderful fruit in the lives of my children, grandchildren, and great-grandchildren. What do you need to do to strengthen or begin to worship God with your family? What challenges do you face to start a family worship experience, and what are you going to do about them?

5. Those who know God well spend daily time with him. How would you rate your time alone with God daily, and what can you do to enrich it?

COMMITMENT

WE ARE NOW AT THE central request of the Prayer Covenant. "Jesus, be Lord of my life today in new ways, and change me any way you want!" This request is an expression of unreserved commitment to the lordship of Christ. When we pray this prayer we are giving the Lord a license over our lives to do whatever he thinks best, no matter what it costs or however inconvenient it may be.

I am excited to tell you the story of how the Prayer Covenant began and how it grew over the years of my ministry. This line once comprised the whole Prayer Covenant, and then it became part of what I have come to call the "short form." While the prayer did grow and develop to what we are exploring in this book, this line of the prayer, "Jesus, be Lord of my life today in new ways, and change me any way you want!" is truly the heart of the Prayer Covenant. Everything you have read about the Prayer Covenant so far leads up to this request, and all that you will read about in the coming chapters flows from it.

"Jesus, be Lord of my life . . ." Jesus announces his lordship when he begins his ministry as he walks into Galilee on his mission from God, declaring, "The kingdom of God has come near. Repent and believe the good news!" (Mark 1:15). Throughout his ministry, Jesus demonstrates his lordship over sickness, demons, nature, and people. When he meets and commissions his disciples after his crucifixion and resurrection, he affirms what he preached and demonstrated throughout his ministry, in the Great Commission: "All authority in heaven and on earth has been given to me" (Matthew 28:18).

Of course Jesus' exercise of authority did not cease when he ascended to heaven—he was and is as active as ever. As the church begins its ministry under the leadership of the apostles,

Jesus as Lord sends the Holy Spirit to empower them. On the day of Pentecost when the Spirit comes on the church in power, Peter says, "God has raised this Jesus to life, and we are all witnesses of the fact. Exalted to the right hand of God, he has received from the Father the promised Holy Spirit and has poured out what you now see and hear" (Acts 2:32-33). The title of what we call Acts could justly be called the Acts of Jesus Christ.

All who believed and entered into the Christian community, the church, were taught about the lordship of Christ:

> In the past God spoke to our ancestors through the prophets at many times and in various ways, but in these last days he has spoken to us by his Son, whom he appointed heir of all things, and through whom he made the universe. The Son is the radiance of God's glory and the exact representation of his being, sustaining all things by his powerful word. After he had provided purification for sins, he sat down at the right hand of the Majesty in heaven. (Hebrews 1:1-3)

This is a stunning statement to make of a human being. Not even the rulers of the classical world, caesars, pharaohs, and emperors who claimed that they were sons of the gods, went as far as this. Nor would Jews schooled in the Old Testament dare to make such a statement, as it was clear that God would not share his glory with another (Isaiah 42:8). Jesus shatters all previous ways of thinking about God, as in him we come face to face with the incarnate God, the second person of the Trinity.

When we get a glimpse of heaven in the book of Revelation, sure enough, there is Jesus, reigning at the right hand of God the Father as ruler of the universe. As the source of all goodness and authority, he is worshiped there. "Then I heard every creature in heaven and on earth and under the earth and on the sea, and all that is in them, saying: 'To him who sits on the throne and to the Lamb be praise and honor and glory and power, for ever and ever!'" (Revelation 5:13).

GETTING STARTED WITH THE LORDSHIP OF CHRIST

As a young pastor, I had much to learn about the lordship of Christ, and God was going to teach me. One of the responsibilities I had as a young pastor in New Wilmington, Pennsylvania, where Westminster College is located, was to be the chair of a committee for evangelism in our part of the state. When I was asked by John Tate, our statewide leader, to give a committee report to pastors and elders representing the entire state, I smiled and gave a challenging answer: "I'll do it if you'll let me do it my way."

"What is your way?" John asked.

I replied, "I don't want to give a committee report. Committee reports bore people. I want to tell about people coming to know Jesus Christ personally. I want to take people with me who are excited about their faith in Jesus and are being used by God to lead others to know Christ and follow him. I want them to tell their stories and sing God's truth in such powerful and contagious ways that by the end of the report, everyone will be so encouraged and inspired that they will respond with a spontaneous joyful ovation to our Lord."

With a twinkle in his eye he said to me, "You give the report."

First, I called Joy and Ed Tobin. Joy had sung the lead in The Sound of Music, and Ed had sung the lead in The Music Man. They were dear friends, lots of fun, and unusually gifted musicians. They were part of a small group that I and my wife, Patty, met with regularly. They said yes to my request and chose to sing songs from the musical For Heaven's Sake. They invited all who were present to sing with them of the experience of God's grace.

Then I went to Linda Pickleseimer, an outstanding pianist and worship leader. She also said yes. Finally, I called Don Rehberg, the controller of J and L Steel in Pittsburgh, with twelve hundred employees under him. He was an elder in his church and a leader within the Pittsburgh Experiment, a Christian nondenominational ministry founded by Sam Shoemaker that provides spiritual resources to business, professional and working people as well as to area churches.

At first, I couldn't get through to Don. But a short time later he returned my call and apologized for not being available earlier. Then he said to me, "Jerry, when you called, I was on my knees with one of my managers, who was giving his life to Christ. I wouldn't have interrupted that for anyone. Why did you call?"

"Don, that's why I called," I said. "God works through you to touch people's lives. He has affected your life profoundly, and he uses you to bring people to know and follow Jesus. I'm asking you to take two days out of your busy schedule and go with me to Wilson College in eastern Pennsylvania. I want you to tell your story. It is a gathering of leading pastors and elders representing every part of the state of Pennsylvania with responsibility for over 400,000 Presbyterians. Will you do that?"

Don said he would think about it. He called back within the hour to say he would be glad to clear his calendar. This, then, was the team.

These people had each blessed my life. I knew their faith and the integrity of their lives. They could sing and tell the good news of Jesus Christ in a winsome and contagious way. And they knew from experience that God is at work today through his people.

The four of us picked up Don at the entrance to the turnpike just outside Pittsburgh on our way to Wilson College. I asked each of them to introduce themselves to one another, including their own story of coming to faith. It was easy to celebrate their friendship and unique gifts.

After they had gotten to know each other, I asked Don if he would share with us what God was doing in his life. Don told the story of going to Music Hall in Pittsburgh to hear Sam Shoemaker's last sermon, "Get Changed—Get Together—and Get Going." Shoemaker encouraged people to get changed by giving your life to Christ, "giving as much of yourself as you can to as much of Christ as you understand." Get together with other growing Christians so that your lives encourage and challenge one another to keep growing in faith and commitment. Then get going by discovering together what God wants to do through you. Don's account gripped our minds and stirred our hearts. As we drove along, Don told one story after another for nearly an hour, because we kept asking him for more.

When we arrived at the conference we were fired up and eager to share. Because of what God did among us as Don shared, I had a new expectation that the Lord was going to do something special the next day when we gave our report. And he did!

PRAYING THE LORDSHIP OF CHRIST

I thought I was going to the synod to give the evangelism report in order to bless others. But God knew I needed to be with Don. I needed a new heart commitment to Jesus Christ as Lord. You may have already guessed where this story is going.

Remember how I opened this book, with the story of joining in a Prayer Covenant with a business leader in Pittsburgh? That man was Don Rehberg! It should already be clear how influential that Prayer Covenant has been in my life. It had an immediate impact on the evangelism report that followed.

When my team members shared their songs and faith and stories, this somewhat reserved group of Presbyterian pastors and elders from every area of Pennsylvania exploded spontaneously into a standing ovation for the Lord. They celebrated the good news of God's grace in Christ and what he is doing through his people now. What a privilege to be part of it!

The ride home was special. We were thankful and very different people. But I had no idea what God had in store for me. I'm not sure what I had been doing as a pastor before that. I loved the Lord and was seeking to preach the Word of God faithfully. I was giving myself to my people day by day, spending considerable time in study, teaching, and counseling. I listened, cared, prayed, and was encouraged by people's growing interest and response to our Lord. The love and fellowship of God's people and the joy of the Lord seemed to be growing among us within the congregation.

But I had not been intentionally and consistently giving my life to Christ as Lord with joy and abandonment at the beginning of each day. Nor had I been inviting people individually to a deeper personal commitment to Christ on a regular basis. I had not been expecting God to transform us continually and use us powerfully day by day to affect the lives of those around us. Prior to that meeting I could not say what Don Rehberg had said to me on the phone when we first talked ("I was on my knees with one of my key managers giving his life to Christ"). It seemed like I had been working for Christ rather than allowing Christ to work through me. To be honest with you and myself, I have had to learn that lesson over and over again.

When we returned home, things changed quickly. I began praying the Prayer Covenant for my life and then for Don each day, and I knew Don was praying for me. I knew God loved to answer this kind of prayer. Now in my ministry I was inviting people to ask Jesus to be Lord of their lives on a regular basis. Almost every person who came for counseling ended up wanting to enter into the Prayer Covenant, and I had an extensive counseling ministry. Most people who came to see me were ready to take this simple but profound step for themselves and then to pray for me. They liked knowing I knew I needed their prayers and love as much as they needed mine. I had assumed that was already true but now knew it in a new way. Now we were "following Jesus together."

THE SHORT FORM OF THE PRAYER COVENANT

When I first started to pray the Prayer Covenant, it was concise. "Jesus, be Lord of my life." That's it! Simple. I prayed it at the beginning of each day, as Don Rehberg suggested. Doing so made sense, as it fit with what I had learned years before with Mike McCutchen, that I needed to start each day by meeting with Jesus.

Before long, I added the word "today." I wanted to keep my commitment fresh and current. I was saying to Jesus, "I am holding nothing back." This is not a prayer of which a person could easily go through the motions. It encouraged me to believe that the Lord had something new and fresh he wanted to teach me.

After I added "today," I then began to pray "in new ways." I wanted to grow on a regular basis. I wanted to be on the cutting edge of growth, and I wanted each day to be a fresh adventure. I was praying it each day in response to Jesus' invitation "to take up my cross daily and follow him." I didn't want to presume that I was already following him without needing to learn and grow.

Next, I added, "Change me any way you want." I knew that the additional phrases could seem redundant, but they didn't feel that way to me. It was like I was saying to the Lord, "I really mean it, Jesus. I want you to have total freedom to change me today with no hesitations, inhibitions, or reservations on my part." Each additional thought was building a greater sense of expectancy within me that God would speak clearly through his Word and Spirit.

So the prayer had grown to this: "Jesus, be Lord of my life today in new ways, and change me any way you want."

And of course, as you are discovering by reading this book, the Prayer Covenant expanded through the years to incorporate ten requests other than just this one. While all the other requests were added for good reasons, this request is the heart of it. I have a friend who invited his wife to enter the Prayer Covenant with him.

Reading over the prayer to see just what she was committing to, she commented when she came upon the line "change me any way you want": "This is a dangerous prayer." It is! Who knows what will happen when we give ourselves over completely to Jesus on a continuing basis? But it is exciting! When we give our lives to Jesus, not even the sky is the limit. I had begun a glorious adventure with the Lord of the universe. The adventure is still growing forty-five years later.

THE SUPREMACY OF CHRIST

The lordship and supremacy of Jesus Christ is something I want to proclaim everywhere. And it is something that needs to be proclaimed everywhere, as it is slipping behind the scenes in much of the church and in the hearts of many sincere believers. David Bryant, in his book *Christ Is All!*, pointed out that in a *Time* magazine article about the church in America in the final decade of the twentieth century, there was not one reference to Jesus Christ. The Christian church, in all its denominations, is very busy about religion, but it is often missing the key because Jesus Christ is not proclaimed and believed supreme. Bryant writes that it isn't even enough to say that Jesus Christ is central. While that might sound good, it still makes Jesus only one of many important things. No! Jesus is not one of many. The Bible is very clear: Jesus is Lord over everything. He is supreme. "And God placed all things under his feet and appointed him to be head over everything for the church, which is his body, the fullness of him who fills everything in every way" (Ephesians 1:22-23).

The little church in Colossae in the first century needed to be reminded of the supremacy of Jesus Christ, too. They were being inundated with false teachers who said, "It is good that you believe in Jesus. But you also need to add other rituals and regulations." "No!" says the apostle Paul. He tells them that Jesus Christ

> is before all things, and in him all things hold together. And he is the head of the body, the church; he is the beginning and the firstborn from among the dead, so that in everything he might have the supremacy. For God was pleased to have all his fullness dwell in him, and through him to reconcile to himself all things, whether things on earth or things in heaven, by making peace through his blood, shed on the cross. (Colossians 1:17-20)

Paul also writes of the supremacy of Christ to Christians in the larger metropolitan church in Ephesus:

> [God] raised Christ from the dead and seated him at his right hand in the heavenly realms, far above all rule and authority, power and dominion, and every name that is invoked, not only in the present age but also in the one to come. And God placed all things under his feet and appointed him to be head over everything. (Ephesians 1:20-22)

In response to faulty conceptions of the lordship of Christ, David Bryant wrote his book to call us all to "join in the joyful awakening to the supremacy of God's Son." He writes with great passion and conviction, inviting all who read it

> to enter into something worthy of your whole heart; an invitation to join a movement already underway. An invitation to start celebrating as a way of life, nothing less than the supremacy

of God's Son for all he is, for you and for me, for now and for the future.[17]

When we pray, "Jesus, be Lord of my life today in new ways, and change me any way you want," we are declaring and surrendering completely to the supremacy of Christ over everything and joining in this joyful movement.

A DANGEROUS AND GRACIOUS PRAYER

This prayer is a dangerous prayer if you mean it. It is wise to think carefully before you pray it. But be encouraged. We can pray it because it is also a prayer of grace.

I was talking about the Prayer Covenant with a friend in California. We had worked together for Christian causes for many years, and I considered him one of my closest friends. We had prayed for each other for years and talked about the Lord on many occasions.

It seemed right to talk with him about the Prayer Covenant and invite him to pray it with me. I went through it line by line and said it would be a great privilege to pray it with him if he wanted to do so. He said that he and his wife were leaving that afternoon for a retreat with other Christian couples and he wanted to think about it for a few weeks. That made sense to me. It is always good for people to think honestly and deeply, even to pray earnestly about whether they are ready to commit their lives to Jesus Christ as Lord and be accountable to another person. There is no way to know ahead of time where this prayer will lead us, and it is important to

---

17 (David Bryant, Christ Is All! [New Providence, NJ: New Providence Publishers, 2010]).

be ready to trust that God will guide.

When I called him a few weeks later he said, "Jerry, I am not ready. I need to think more about it. I can pray all of the prayer except those words: 'Jesus, be Lord of my life today in new ways, and change me any way you want.' If I pray that prayer I will be out of control. I don't know where it will lead me."

I laughed. I said, "You are right. That's the whole point of the prayer: We are saying, 'Jesus, we want you to be in control.' We are saying we trust our lives to you. We want your will no matter where it leads us." I expanded on this with a frank challenge. "In this prayer we are saying to Jesus, 'We believe that if we allow you to be in charge of our day and of our future that it will be well with our soul. It will be well with our destiny here on earth and for eternity. We are saying that we believe you, Jesus, can do a better job in and through our lives than we can.'"

Then I said to him, "I don't struggle with the prayer. That is my heart's desire and has been for a long time. I want Jesus to lead me. What I struggle with is knowing whether my life is consistent with the prayer. What I struggle with is understanding all that the prayer should produce in me."

With these words, he came alive on the phone. He said, "Jerry, do you struggle with that? Are you not sure you are living what you pray? After knowing the Lord for over sixty years, are you telling me that you still struggle with being sure you are living a life consistent with the prayer?"

I laughed again. "Of course I struggle with that. The more I pray this prayer, and the more I seek to follow Jesus and allow him to live his life in me, the more aware I become of how far I fall short, and how much I need him and his mercy and the power of the Spirit. I want him to change me from the inside out. The Prayer Covenant is 'the set of the sail,' a matter of the heart, not a matter of perfect implementation. Jesus did it perfectly. We never do. He alone can live the Christian life by living his life within us."

"Oh," he replied. "Then I can pray the prayer. I am ready to enter into the Prayer Covenant with you. I want Jesus to be Lord. But I never fully measure up." Then he volunteered, "By the way, I serve on the board of the largest Christian radio network in America. This coming week I've been asked to lead devotions for the board meeting. I've been struggling with what I ought to share. In the middle of the night the words 'flat out' came to me. Do you think they could have meaning for me and the board meeting?"

I replied, "I believe the timing of our conversation is a 'God-thing.' 'Flat out' is the meaning of the Prayer Covenant. We are saying, 'Jesus, be Lord of my life today, and change me any way you want.' We are saying, 'I am ready to hold nothing back and to live flat out for you, Jesus. I want your will. I want your glory. I want to live for you.' Does that make sense to you?"

"Yes," he replied. "That makes lots of sense to me. And because you have shared your own struggle with me, I feel free to share God's call and my own struggle with the board."

So, be assured, the lordship of Christ is a lordship of grace. We don't pray this prayer because we are perfect, but because he is and we know we are not.

THE CALL OF JESUS

When Jesus announced the coming of the kingdom of God, he called his disciples. "Come, follow me," Jesus said, "and I will send you out to fish for people" (Mark 1:17). The disciples responded and surrendered to the lordship of Jesus Christ. Forever after they lived under his authority. Not perfectly, but genuinely. It was their new way of life. It is to be our new way of life as well. Some people think that they surrendered to Jesus when they first believed, and now they can get on with their lives as they choose. That is not how it works. He is Lord, and we are to live daily under the lordship of Christ.

> "Therefore, my dear friends, as you have always obeyed—not only in my presence, but now much more in my absence—continue to work out your salvation with fear and trembling, for it is God who works in you to will and to act in order to fulfill his good purpose" (Philippians 2:12-13).

Just as we discovered in the previous chapter that the worship of God is a joyful work, so submitting to the lordship of Christ is a joyful work as well. Daryl Guider wrote a book entitled *The Continuing Conversion of the Church*. He points out that our conversion is not just a one-time thing; it is continuing as we daily surrender to the lordship of Jesus Christ. This surrender means many things, but central to it is our commitment to obedience. We want to obey him. We pray to obey him.

Eugene Peterson, the author of *The Message* translation, wrote about this in one of his first books, *A Long Obedience in the Same Direction*. We keep at it all our lives. This obedience is not a burden but freedom and a thrill. Jesus told those who were considering his call: "Come to me, all you who are weary and burdened, and I will give you rest. Take my yoke upon you and learn from me, for I am gentle and humble in heart, and you will find rest for your souls. For my yoke is easy, and my burden is light" (Matthew 11:28-30).

CHRIST IS ALL!

It truly is all about Jesus. I invite you to think about what you have learned about the Prayer Covenant so far and what we will pray in the rest of the book.

1. First we pray in gratitude for God's grace and love that come to us through Jesus Christ.

2. Then we ask for the grace to be able to love him without compromise or equivocation.

3. Next we pray to be empowered to love others.

4. We then receive the forgiveness of God, which comes to us through the death of Jesus Christ and our response of repentance.

5. Having been forgiven we respond to God's grace to us through Jesus Christ by grateful worship.

6. Having considered the heart of the Prayer Covenant, the lordship of Jesus Christ, we will now turn our attention to the rest of the prayer:

7. We pray for dependence on the Holy Spirit, which Jesus sends to his people.

8. We pray to be instruments of God to influence others in the world to obey Jesus Christ.

9. We pray that we will grow to be able to invite others to follow Jesus as Lord together.

10. Finally we seal our prayer by praying in the authority of Jesus' name.

When we pray, "Jesus, be Lord of my life today in new ways, and change me any way you want," we are "joining in the joyful awakening to the supremacy of God's Son," a movement already under way, and one that we pray will sweep this country and the world.

REFLECTION QUESTIONS

Chapter 7   Commitment

1. This request is the heart of the Prayer Covenant. What comes to mind when you hear the phrase, "The Lordship and supremacy of Christ"?

2. Sometimes spiritual practices can become binding laws— legalistic. As you pray this prayer of commitment, what difference can it make to remember that God is gracious?

3. Spiritual passions may cool and we aren't even aware of it. How would you describe the zest and constancy of your following Christ as Lord today and recent months?

4. This request which includes the phrase "change me anyway you want" has been described as "dangerous." What is dangerous about it?

5. I find this request exciting and adventurous because it continually brings me into deeper relationship with the sovereign Lord of the universe. How could it be exciting and adventurous for you?

CHAPTER 8

DEPENDENCE

HAVING MADE UNRESERVED COMMITMENT TO the Lord as we prayed for Jesus to be Lord of our lives, our prayer turns to a declaration of dependence by requesting and receiving the gift that Jesus promised to us: the Holy Spirit. In this line of the Prayer Covenant, we pray, "Fill me with your Holy Spirit," because we can only fulfill our commitment to Jesus as Lord by the power of the Holy Spirit. Although we are seldom conscious of it, our life is dependent upon the air we breathe. In the same way, we may not be conscious of it, but our spiritual life is dependent upon the Spirit of God.

How do we get filled with the Holy Spirit? Why should we pray for it?

It is important to know that there are many different ministries of the Spirit. The Holy Spirit convicts us of sin (John 16:8), enlightens us (John 16:13-16), grants us the gift of repentance (Acts 11:15-18), regenerates us into new life, and then leads us into a holy life that is pleasing to God—we call this sanctification (Romans 8:5-8). He works in us individually as well as in a community, empowering us for mission and leading us in worship. The Spirit comes to us in different ways and in different times for the different purposes of God. Just as we must drink water to quench the thirst of our bodies, we must also drink of the Spirit to quench the thirst of our souls.

In his book *The Holy Spirit: Activating God's Power in Your Life*, Billy Graham reminds us that Jesus brought eternal life. It is the Holy Spirit who brings internal life. He indwells us, truly inhabiting our bodies. It can be a shock when you think about the fact that if you are a follower of Jesus Christ, there is more than one person within you. It is one of the mysteries of God that while Jesus is bodily at the right hand of God, he also lives in our hearts by the indwelling of the Holy Spirit (Ephesians 3:17). Jesus explains to the disciples that he was not going to leave them as orphans, even though he was going to be crucified and then ascend to heaven. Jesus promises that he will come to them and indwell them by means of the Spirit (John 14:17-18).

Especially in the hours before his crucifixion, Jesus spoke repeatedly of the many ministries of the Holy Spirit in John 14–16. Jesus told the disciples that the Spirit would not only be with them but also in them. The Spirit would be in them as the counselor, comforter, guide, advocate, and teacher. He would also be the power behind their mission, cutting right through the resistance of the hardhearted world. Jesus promised them that his departure, ironically, was going to be good for his disciples, because it would bring the presence and power of God through the coming of the Holy Spirit: "But I tell you the truth: It is for your good that I am going away. Unless I go away, the Counselor will not come to you; but if I go, I will send him to you" (John 16:7).

THE REGENERATING WORK OF THE SPIRIT

Two images of the Holy Spirit in the Bible are fire and light. Moses was attracted by the burning bush that was never incinerated, and the Holy Spirit came at Pentecost with "tongues of fire" (Acts 2:3). Fire not only warms—it also brings light. Even so, the Holy Spirit brings light and enlightens us. The two disciples walking with Jesus on the road to Emmaus still didn't understand Jesus until their eyes were opened by the Holy Spirit. "Were not our hearts burning within us while he talked with us on the road and opened the Scriptures to us?" (Luke 24:32). This enlightening of the Spirit is not magical. It is woven into the experiences of life and the evidences God gives us.

> What the Holy Spirit does in the new birth is not to make a man a Christian regardless of the evidence, but on the contrary to clear away the mists from his eyes and enable him to attend to the evidence.[18]

The story of the Trabert family is a wonderful illustration of how the Holy Spirit works to open us up to Jesus Christ, bringing us to new life even as he challenges us to surrender. Doris Trabert, whom you'll recall I mentioned in an earlier chapter, was a member of College Hill and on fire for the Lord. We started a couples group that included Doris and her husband, Marc. The Traberts stood out to me not only because of Doris's outstanding faith but also because Marc's brother Tony had been my idol during my college years. Tony had been ranked the top tennis player in the world and had won three of the four majors—the French Open, Wimbledon, and the U.S. Open—all in the same year. I wanted to be a great tennis player, just like Tony, but it was not to be.

Although Doris was an outstanding Christian, Marc was not a believer. It was because Doris hoped I might lead Marc to the Lord that I invited them to join the couples group. Marc, while not a believer, was a good sport about Doris's involvement at College Hill. He became involved in the Teen Breakfast Club, cooking eggs and bacon for high school kids, a group that grew to three hundred and then to seven hundred. Marc also became a leader in our Friday morning men's Bible study group, meeting in the home of Phil and Marianne Wheeler, which grew from an intimate group of

18 (J. Gresham Machen, The Christian Faith in the Modern World [Grand Rapids, MI: Eerdmans, 1947], p. 63).

four to over a hundred each Friday at 6:30 a.m.

During that time I was asked to lead a preaching mission at Bay Village Presbyterian Church outside Cleveland. I took thirty people with me to bear witness. Marc was one I asked to go, even though I knew that he didn't know the Lord. Marc was surprised, of course, and said to me, "You don't have to ask me so you can get Doris to go."

I replied, "I am not asking you for Doris's sake. I am asking you to go and tell your story and where you are with Jesus and what you are doing and what you are learning."

Marc said, "You know I have only let Jesus in the front door, but I haven't signed over the deed of the house."

"Marc, I know that," I replied. "You are in worship every Sunday, you come to our couples group, you get up at 4:30 a.m. on Thursdays to cook breakfast for teenagers, and you have the wonderful ability to be real and transparent. About not yet having given your life to Christ, I can tell you there are people at the church we are going to who think they are dedicated Christians, and yet they are not half as involved as you are. Many at this church will relate to you."

After meetings all weekend, about ninety people gathered to share what the weekend had meant to them. Many were blessed incredibly by the entire group. But the person most referred to, by far, was Marc Trabert.

Marc and Doris were part of 120 people who went out to Trail West, a Young Life facility for adults, the following summer. It was a great week. On Thursday night we visited Frontier Ranch, where Young Life was conducting their camp for teenagers from around the country. The message was on the cross of Christ and Jesus' readiness to come into our lives. After the meeting, my wife, Patty, and I were walking around the grounds. Marc came up to me and threw his arms around me and said, "I did it. I gave my life to Jesus Christ and I am his." In the days that followed we could all see the difference. Doris and Marc were filled with love, and their daughters were transformed in the years to come. Immediately Marc began to have an impact on the men who came to the Friday morning Bible study. He challenged us all to live godly lives. He was holding nothing back.

The enlightening work of the Spirit continued in the Trabert family. Marc wanted his famous tennis champion brother, Tony, to meet Christ, and he shared his faith on more than one occasion. But six months after signing over the deed of his heart to Christ, Marc was killed in a plane crash with three other business leaders heading to Florida for a golf outing.

But that is not the end of the story. The Holy Spirit works in amazing ways. Doris not only prayed for each of her daughters but for years she prayed daily for Tony. When she died, her daughters asked me to lead her memorial service. Jenny, one of Doris's daughters, said to me "Please make the gospel clear, because Uncle Tony is coming to the service, and he needs to meet Christ." I said to her, "I want him to meet Christ, too, and I will share the gospel, but please don't lay that on me. Only Jesus brings people to himself, by his Spirit. I can't do that. You pray. Pray for me, and pray that the Spirit will touch Tony. But we need to leave Tony in the Lord's hands." In an age in which we are repeatedly told we must depend on ourselves—our own efforts and our own capabilities—God's people must continually recall that we are dependent not on ourselves alone but on God's Spirit.

Tony and his wife were sitting in the front pew as people were coming for the visitation. I had prayed for him throughout the years, but in a limited way, certainly not like Doris had prayed for him. Years earlier, Tony had asked me if I would lead his memorial service when his time came. I said I would but only if he would let me prepare him for death. Up until that point, I had sent him a book or two, but we had very little contact. At this funeral for Doris, he was not sure about faith and life and death. So I asked him if he would like to go into my former office and have a little private time together. He said yes, and so we chatted for a time and then returned to the front pew of the sanctuary. I could tell that he didn't know many of the people. I again invited him back into my former study before the service began. Up until that point, it hadn't seemed natural for me to raise the question of his relationship to the Lord. But it seemed very natural the second time we were alone together. I talked to him about Jesus, and about God's love for him. I asked, "Would you like to look at a verse of Scripture with me?" He was quick to say yes.

I opened to Revelation 3:20: "Here I am! I stand at the door and knock. If anyone hears my voice and opens the door, I will come in and eat with him, and he with me." Then I said, "Tony, who do you think is knocking?"

"Jesus," he replied.

"Yes," I said. "Where do you think he is knocking?"

"At my heart."

"Yes. He says, 'If anyone hears my voice and opens the door...'

"How do you think we hear God's voice?"

THE PRAYER COVENANT Dependence

He wasn't sure, so I went on. "Sometimes we hear through Scripture, or a friend or a pastor, and sometimes we hear his voice through the death of a brother. What do you think it means to open the door?"

"I've got to do something."

"What do you have to do?"

"I need to open myself to him."

"Yes. You need to open yourself. The promise of Christ is that he will come into your heart and life if you open the door of your heart. Is there any reason for putting this off any longer?"

"No."

"Do you want to do this now?

"Yes!"

Would it help if I suggested what you might pray line by line?"

"Yes."

So I led him in prayer and shared with him the short version of the Prayer Covenant. I then discipled him over the phone on a weekly basis for more than a year. I never knew two brothers who were more connected than Marc and Tony. I am sure that part of the reason he prayed to receive Christ was that he wanted to be with his brother in eternity.

It has been a privilege to see the redemptive power of God at work in that family. I knew that only the Holy Spirit could open up Tony's heart to Christ. I also knew that Doris had prayed for him daily for many, many years. I knew that his three nieces had been praying for him for years. And I also knew that the Holy Spirit works through prayer. That is why the Prayer Covenant is so powerful. God uses people who are open to his Spirit, who are dependent on his Spirit, and who are filled with his Spirit.

SPIRITUAL BREATHING

The Greek word for *spirit* literally means "air." Just as air is all around us and in us, so the Holy Spirit is around us and in us. The Holy Spirit brings the fresh air of heaven. It makes sense that we would be filled with the Spirit by learning to "breathe the Spirit." Bill Bright, the founder and leader of Campus Crusade for many years, used to talk about breathing spiritually. He said that we breathe in new spiritual air, new life, and new vigor by asking and believing God to "fill us with his Holy Spirit." He loved to point out that the apostle Paul in Ephesians 5:18-19 calls us to be filled with God's Spirit, and the verb he used means to be filled on a continual basis.

We live in the Spirit by continually breathing in and out spiritually, so that there are no lingering sins to rob us of our freedom and strength in the Lord. This two-part process—of breathing out spiritually through confession and repentance, then breathing in by asking God to fill us with his Spirit—is God's wonderful provision of continual inward renewal and transformation. After we release our sin to the Lord, we are ready to be filled with God's Spirit by God himself.

I had the privilege of speaking along with Bill Bright at a number of prayer and fasting conferences. At each he shared the same message about spiritual breathing. At first I wondered whether he had forgotten that he had already shared these truths. But then it became clear. He had not forgotten. He knew that this message is so important and essential that everyone desperately needs to know these truths in a way that continually transforms their lives. The apostle Paul, along with Bill Bright, wanted to be sure all of us would receive the presence and power of God on a regular basis by being filled with God's Spirit.

The power of God comes flowing into us through the Holy Spirit. Another image that God uses to help us understand the power of the Spirit is wind. When Jesus speaks to Nicodemus, he says, "The wind blows wherever it pleases. You hear its sound, but you cannot tell where it comes from or where it is going. So it is with everyone born of the Spirit" (John 3:8). We see the Spirit as wind in other passages, too: hovering over the waters at creation (Genesis 1:2), and poured out on the church at Pentecost as the believers hear "the blowing of a violent wind" (Acts 2:2). There is power in the air. It can be quiet and gentle, as well as thunderous and overwhelming.

THE SANCTIFYING WORK OF THE HOLY SPIRIT

The Spirit nourishes us so that we grow in godliness and produce the fruit of the Spirit. When we are filled with the Spirit, people will find that we "taste good" as the Spirit works the character of Jesus within us—love, joy, peace, patience, kindness, goodness, faithfulness, gentleness, and self-control (Galatians 5:22-23). This fruit of the Spirit is what we are all hungry for as God nourishes souls and enriches whole congregations.

The Spirit works on us, around us, and inside us. J. B. Phillips, in his groundbreaking paraphrase of Acts, makes this point in his introduction:

> People were unquestionably being changed at the root of their being: cowards become heroes; sinners are transformed; fear, greed, envy and pride are expelled by a flood of something above and beyond normal human experience... the cruel, the wicked, the evil-minded and the God-less become filled with self love... and generous courage.[19]

We want to be filled with the Spirit because the Spirit brings the presence of God and all his blessings. Jonathan Edwards, a great teacher used powerfully by the Holy Spirit in the *First Great Awakening*, wrote:

> It is through the vital communications and indwellings of the Spirit that the saints have all their light, life, holiness, beauty and joy in heaven; and it is through the vital communications and indwelling of the same Spirit that the saints have all light, life, holiness, beauty and comfort on earth; but only communicated in less measure.[20]

THE SPIRIT, THE RENEWAL MOVEMENT AND THE CHARISMATIC MOVEMENT

Writing about the Holy Spirit raises the issue of the gifts of the Spirit, and so I want to touch on these. I have had many positive

---

19 (J. B. Phillips, The Young Church in Action [New York: Macmillan, 1957], preface, p. x).
20 (Jonathan Edwards, Religious Affections [Carlisle, PA: Banner of Truth Trust, 1958], p. 162)

experiences with people who would call themselves charismatic and Pentecostals. I have seen how God has blessed through the gifts, even though I never entered into the gift of tongues. For a period of time in the '60s and '70s the power of the Spirit was discovered in fresh ways around the country as I was beginning my pastoral ministry. There was a lot of controversy about spiritual gifts, and I came to the conclusion that we don't need to be afraid nor defensive about the Holy Spirit. Further, I came to the conclusion that we shouldn't put each other into boxes, either.

Bruce Larson, a pastor, author, and leader within the national Renewal Movement, came to visit Mt. Lebanon Church with a team of fifteen people. Bruce had this natural way of transparency and vulnerability that allowed Jesus to use him to touch people's lives. The team he brought with him was amazing, too. They were joyful, equally transparent, and in love with Jesus Christ. I thought I had invited them for the sake of the congregation, but I was already in danger of becoming a professional churchman—I had begun to lose the freedom and power of the Spirit. I was touched and transformed that weekend by what Bruce and his team said and by who they were. The Spirit was alive in them and through them and brought the fresh wind of renewal to my life. Someone said to me after that weekend, "It is almost like you have become a new person." I knew they were right, but it hurt my pride to have them say so.

Remember, this was the time when the charismatic movement of the Spirit was sweeping into many mainline churches across the country. One congregation in our town was swept up, too. In New Wilmington there were two Presbyterian churches. I served the church across the street from Westminster College, and the other was about six blocks away. The other pastor, reserved and scholarly, entered into the gift of tongues, which was considered by many to be the "sign gift"—evidence of receiving the Holy Spirit. His experience of the Holy Spirit liberated him in ways that were evident and surprising. Several students who had been worshiping at my church now began to go to the other Presbyterian church. Then one of the college professors who worshiped with us began to encourage the charismatic gifts of the Spirit. I celebrated their newfound spiritual vitality.

Some college students who were touched by the professor who had received tongues met with me to share their experience. They asked if they could pray over me. One of them asked me "Are you filled with the Spirit?" I answered yes. Then he asked, "Are you sure?" I said, "I was until you asked me." I thought about that conversation a lot. It was an important part of the process that challenged me to give attention to the Spirit in ways that I had never before considered.

Then another professor and a business leader in town, both members of my congregation, became involved in the charismatic movement as well. They were on my elder board and began to share their stories with me in hopes that I would join in what they felt was this new and wonderful work of God's Spirit. I was open to them because I saw deep needs met in their lives and new strengths developed in them. They were growing spiritually and showed an even deeper commitment to our congregation.

THE SPIRIT AND HEALING

The work of the Spirit was certainly the spirit of the time. I had just accepted my call to College Hill when one of the leading young people visited a youth group in another church and entered into the gifts of the Holy Spirit and tongues. I said to my wife, "Can you believe this? I have been here one month and the gifts of the Spirit are already breaking out here as they did in New Wilmington."

I was very open to the gifts of the Spirit and his work of healing, which seemed to accompany the charismatic movement. I believed that God was still in the healing ministry according to what I read in James: "Is any one among you sick? He should call the elders of the church to pray over him and anoint him with oil in the name of the Lord. And the prayer offered in faith will make the sick person well; the Lord will raise him up" (James 5:14-15).

I wanted to participate in the healing ministry because I believed it was faithful to Scripture. However, I found this difficult because of the TV presence and persona of Oral Roberts. At that time Roberts was very well known and the face of the charismatic healing ministry in the country. When most people thought of the healing work of the Spirit, they thought of him. However, his style was not very Presbyterian, and not my style. But I did believe that God was still in the healing ministry. That openness is what led me to begin a healing ministry at New Wilmington and eventually to seek healing for my own sense of inadequacy.

My confidence in the healing ministry of the Holy Spirit continued to grow. Toward the end of my first year as pastor at College Hill, I asked if the session/elder board would like to study the biblical basis for the ministry of healing and bring back recommendations. They said yes, so I worked with that committee, which eventually recommended that we begin a monthly healing service with elders and pastors serving together.

That first healing service began the same week my mother and father arrived for a visit from Seattle. My mother had a form of cancer that attacked her blood platelets. She was serving at that time in the House of Representatives in the state of Washington. She had become so ill that she had to receive blood platelet infusions twice a week. She was so weak she could not bend over to fill a dishwasher.

I spoke to her of the passage in James about God's healing through elders laying on hands and anointing with oil and prayer. This was not her accustomed way to think about the Spirit, or of the way that God worked, so I wasn't sure how she would respond. I said, "Mom, I would love to have you come to the service, but I don't want you to feel any pressure from me." But she was eager to come. We laid hands on her. The outcome? She ceased needing to have platelet infusions for two or three years and was able to serve two more terms in the House of Representatives!

Harry and Elizabeth Causey were also at that first healing service at College Hill. Harry was our worship and choir leader. The couple had tried to have children for a couple of years with no success. Like my mother and many others at the church, they were not accustomed to expect God's Spirit to work in ways that brought healing. Even though they struggled with the idea of a healing service, they were eager to receive the laying on of hands, anointing with oil, and prayer. Ten months later, they gave birth to their first child, David.

These experiences and many other answers to prayer helped us grow in our confidence of the Spirit's healing power. This all contributed to my being open to the validity of all the gifts of the Spirit. In addition, College Hill called a new associate pastor who believed in and experienced all the gifts of the Spirit, and he began to influence members of the church in that direction. As the charismatic movement brought new awareness of the Spirit, there were about two hundred members among our two thousand who received these special gifts. This brought exciting and fresh spiritual vitality to our church.

The Episcopal priest Dennis Bennett was well known for his involvement in the charismatic renewal. He had written *Nine O'clock in the Morning*, the story of what took place in his church in Van Nuys, California, after he preached a Sunday morning sermon about the underground Pentecostal movement that was quietly racing through so many churches in America. When he announced that he himself had spoken in tongues, there was an instant reaction in his church. The story was carried in local newspapers, various wire services picked it up, and the news swept the country. *Time* magazine carried the story. So did *Newsweek*. Dennis and some of his leaders laid hands on me and prayed over me, but I never received the gift of a prayer language. By this time three of our senior staff had. I could see that those who were receptive and received this work of the Spirit grew in their faith, humility, and their effectiveness in leadership.

THE CONTROVERSY OF THE SPIRIT

As the presence of the work of the Spirit in our church became very obvious, there was danger of a potential split between the "haves" and the "have-nots." There were some among the charismatics who became an in-group and assumed that they had a unique role among us, with some sense of superiority and spiritual pride. They presumed everybody should have the spiritual gifts they had received. Some of them considered those who had not received to be less-committed Christians. All in all, this was a relatively small group. On the other hand, there were those who were fearful of the gifts of the Spirit and did not recognize the depth of worship and faith that our charismatic members brought to the fellowship of the entire congregation. Some people just didn't know what to think and felt intimidated, alienated, and defensive.

In response to this potential conflict, I taught on the danger of what I called the *charismaniacs* and *charisphobiacs*—referring to those who were extreme in being for and against the special works of the Spirit. This sermon then led to a four-week series of sermons on the Holy Spirit and a four-week series of classes on the Holy Spirit. We used Charles Hummel's book *Fire in the Fire Place* for our textbook. We had both charismatics and noncharismatics bear witness to the blessings of the Holy Spirit and what they believed was necessary to be able to serve one another together. This movement of the Spirit gave birth to tremendous synergism. Through the Lord our congregation grew during my twenty-year pastorate from less than a thousand in worship to nearly seventeen hundred, with four weekly services—two in the fellowship hall and two in the sanctuary. It was a great privilege for me to see God deepen our unity and overcome the potential charismaniac and charisphobiac split.

What the Spirit did in the life of the church was to deepen our love for each other and our faith, in the presence and power of God at work in the lives of those who were yielded to Christ as Lord. The Spirit was breaking out with gifts all over the place. I was speaking at a Presbyterian event in St. Louis with John McKay, president of Princeton Seminary. After my talk I was approached by a man who said to me, "You are one of us, aren't you?" "Yes!" I said, and then asked, "What are we?" I found myself in a very interesting position: believing in the gifts and ministries of the Spirit but having never received a prayer language nor spoken in tongues.

During that exciting time I was chairman of the Billy Graham Crusade for Cincinnati. As we were preparing for the crusade, we decided to have a preparatory weekend conference. We were amazed that two thousand people registered for this weekend event. Among those who came were keynote speakers Leighton Ford, Tom Skinner, and David du Plessis. The group of speakers was racially diverse and included a mix of charismatics and noncharismatics. The executive committee wanted to emphasize our unity under Jesus' lordship rather than our differences. I met with these speakers ahead of time and stressed, "While all of us love the Lord, we don't agree on all the gifts of the Holy Spirit. We don't agree on tongues. So I ask you to be very careful and focus on our agreement on Jesus and his lordship." They agreed.

However, one of the speakers did not keep his commitment. During the closing meeting he told the entire assembly that, without the special anointing of the Spirit associated with the gift of tongues, the crusade would not have the blessing of God. This was a potential disaster which could possibly fragment all the churches that had joined to participate in our citywide outreach. At the close of that message, I had to confront this distinguished Christian leader in front of the entire group and ask him to apologize for not keeping covenant with our agreement. He graciously apologized and humbly asked our forgiveness—which was given. This was very stressful. However, even those who were upset with me for what appeared to be a public humiliation of a favorite Christian leader affirmed my action and led their people to understand why it was necessary.

Had I not been in the flow of the charismatic movement, I don't believe I could have confronted him.

To this day I love to worship with mature charismatics. And the charismatic movement at College Hill was so mature. I think especially of two elders who were not emotional sorts—one a scientist and the other an engineer. They were thoughtful, methodical, and wholeheartedly charismatic. They brought such wisdom and depth, as did so many others who were open to the filling of the Spirit in whatever way he chose to show himself.

FILLED WITH THE SPIRIT

We have explored some of the images of the Spirit in the Scriptures: fire, light, air, and wind. Another image of the Holy Spirit is water.

> On the last and greatest day of the Feast, Jesus stood and said in a loud voice, "If anyone is thirsty, let him come to me and drink. Whoever believes in me, as the Scripture has said, streams of living water will flow from within him." By this he meant the Spirit, whom those who believed in him were later to receive. Up to that time the Spirit had not been given, since Jesus has not yet been glorified. (John 7:37-39)

For many years these were my life verses. I read them frequently and shared them with others. I wanted the Holy Spirit to flow through me to bring refreshment everywhere I had an opportunity to minister. We all have a deep spiritual thirst, whether we know it or not, that can only be quenched by the Holy Spirit.

I became aware of these wonderful verses during my first year of pastoring, when I was minister of youth at Mt. Lebanon. Cary Weisiger was the senior pastor. In early September I was leading the Labor Day weekend youth retreat at Camp Fairfield with 120 high school and college students, and Cary came to give the closing message. He spoke on John 7:37-39 (RSV) and rivers of living water. He said to us, "The promise of God in your life and through your life is rivers of living water. Not streams, not creeks, but rivers, and they are rivers of living water." He added, "Isn't it amazing how hard some of us work for just a little trickle?"

That rang a bell with me! I worked hard. I had high energy. As far as I could see, I was just getting a little trickle. After hearing that message I went out under the stars to pray. I told God, "Whatever you need to do to change me to release the power of the Holy Spirit through me, I plead with you, change me." That was a pivotal prayer in my life because there is such a contrast when we are trying to work for God rather than allowing God to work through us. Just as a child has to learn to walk and become "independent," we must learn, step by step, to become dependent upon the Spirit, looking to the Spirit, resting in the Spirit, and waiting on the Spirit. This dependence on the Spirit creates sensitivity to God and takes us to deeper levels of both maturity and power.

We are to seek to be filled with the Spirit all the time, as a way of life. Ephesians 5:18 literally says, "Keep on being filled with the Spirit." Think of a sink with a continuous stream of water from the spring outside an old farmhouse. The water, by running constantly, keeps the sink full to the brim with fresh water, both to drink and to use in household chores. In the same way, a Christian is to constantly allow the fresh flow of the Spirit into the soul—for a cool drink and for the chores of the Christian life.

CONCLUSION

I want to remind you that the Prayer Covenant is not magical. It is not automatic. We can pray the prayer and not be changed at all. But we cannot pray the prayer from our heart and with dependence on the Holy Spirit and not be profoundly changed.

We cannot be thankful to God our Father for his grace that made us one of his dearly loved children without growing in his grace and love. We cannot love God with all our heart and love others the way he loves us without being changed at the center of our being. We cannot believe that we are washed clean from every sin without knowing the joy of forgiveness and a clean heart. We cannot praise the Lord with all our heart without being lifted into the presence of God. We cannot pray the prayer "fill me with your Spirit" with the knowledge of Jesus' supremacy and not grow in faith and expectancy. And we can't do any of this without the Holy Spirit. God does not intend us to do so.

The Prayer Covenant is a means, not of magical power but of spiritual power, that brings spiritual life, spiritual character, spiritual ministry, and spiritual gifts. It is not surprising that in those days between his resurrection and ascension Jesus reminded the disciples of his promise: "But you will receive power when the Holy Spirit comes on you; and you will be my witnesses in Jerusalem, and in all Judea and Samaria, and to the ends of the earth" (Acts 1:8).

God's plan is that the Christian life be a joy-filled life. We want to be filled up with God's love—more than that, with God himself! Just as we fill our lungs with air by breathing, and we quench our thirst by drinking, we are filled with the Spirit as we allow him to flow into us. We make our declaration of dependence as we pray, "Jesus, fill me with your Holy Spirit."

REFLECTION QUESTIONS

Chapter 8   Dependence

1. We pray to be filled daily with the Holy Spirit, because like the air we breathe, we can't live without him. Here is a challenging question to begin your reflections on this chapter: we don't pray for daily "air", why do you think we should pray daily to be filled with the Holy Spirit?

2. What are the various ministries of the Holy Spirit? Of which ministry of the Holy Spirit are you most aware and of which ministry of the Holy Spirit are you least aware?

3. There are various images used for the Holy Spirit in the scriptures: air, wind, water, fire, light are those mentioned in this chapter. Reflect on each one and consider; how do those images add to your understanding and experience of the Spirit?

4. Spiritual gifts and spiritual fruit are two different ways that we see the work of the Spirit in our lives and in the church. What are some of the ways you catch glimpses of both spiritual gifts and spiritual fruit in growing Christians around you and in your church?

5. The Holy Spirit enables people to become holy. In what ways are you aware of God shaping and forming your character?

CHAPTER 9
INFLUENCE

NOW THAT WE HAVE ASKED God's Holy Spirit to fill us, we want God to use us for his purpose and be a godly influence, so we pray, "Make me an instrument of your grace, truth, forgiveness, righteousness, and justice." Many of us want to make a difference in the world—to make it better. I believe that through the Lord and by means of prayer, I am able to share in making this world a better place as well as give a foretaste of even better things to come.

INSTRUMENT

In this chapter we are going to take each of these five powerful words in turn—*grace, truth, forgiveness, righteousness,* and *justice.* As light shining through a prism is refracted into multiple colors, so the Holy Spirit, as he is refracted through our lives, manifests himself in multiple expressions of ministry. Before we consider each of these words, we need to pause to reflect on the first part of our request, to be an *instrument* of God. When we ask God to make us an instrument, we are acknowledging that God is the initiator; it all starts with him.

At one time I had used the word *channel* rather than instrument. I changed to the word *instrument*, however, because the word channel does not have enough of the initiative, responsibility, and partnership that God extends to us. The word channel accents the fact that God's work comes through us—we are the conduits. This is good as far as it goes. But we are more than channels: we are agents. We work with God and for God. We are created to participate with him in the ongoing creation and cultivation of his world.

We never know what will happen when we ask God to make us

his instrument. I learned about the pleasure and joy of being an instrument of God as a one-year-old Christian in my first year on the work crew at Silver Cliff, a camping facility for Young Life. After we had finished our chores one evening, we were invited to sit in on a meeting in which Bob Munger, pastor of First Presbyterian of Berkeley, California, was to speak to the national Young Life staff.

He delivered a message that became the wonderful booklet *My Heart, Christ's Home.* Munger described each of our lives as a house. He urged us to invite Jesus into each room inside us. From our living room to the bedroom, and every nook and cranny, he challenged us to open up each part of our lives to the Lord. He invited us to sign over the deed to the heart-house once Jesus had been throughout, because everything about us belongs to him. After that talk, Si Burris, the camp wrangler, and I left the meeting, went to his quarters over the corral, and did just that. We signed over the deeds of our lives. That inspired us to get up early each morning and go out on a rock to read Scripture and pray together.

After a few weeks of early morning meetings, we decided to ride horses up the mountainside for an adventure. On that ride we discovered the Round-Up Lodge for Boys. It was amazing—designed for affluent kids from the Eastern states to spend the summer in an Old West setting. Silver Cliff was good, but this facility was fantastic! What a great tool it could be to expand the ministry of Young Life. We remembered the promise of Jesus recorded in John 14:12-13: "I tell you the truth, anyone who has faith in me will do what I have been doing. He will do even greater things than these, because I am going to the Father. And I will do whatever you ask in my name, so that the Son may bring glory to the Father." That prepared us to pray and claim that camp for Young Life. It was exciting to pray a big prayer to our big God, and we committed ourselves to pray faithfully. I was nineteen and Si was twenty-two.

Jim Rayburn, the founder and president of Young Life, heard about these two students who were praying for the Round-Up Lodge for Boys. A supporter of Young Life then wrote to Jim Rayburn that he had come across a notice in a magazine that the Round-Up Lodge was for sale for $350,000. "Let's go together and buy it," he wrote to Jim. Now, neither he nor Jim Rayburn had any spare money. But the vision and simple prayer led Jim to go to the Young Life Board and ask them whether he would be free to raise the funds. The board said yes. But there was one condition: the funds had to be raised from new donors or enlarged gifts, not existing ones.

So Jim did just that. As he went around the country fundraising, he told the story of the two young men who were praying that God would provide this wonderful facility for the expanding ministry of Young Life. This little step of faith prepared the way, and God did provide the funds. Young Life purchased it, and it became Frontier Ranch, a place where thousands of young people have come to faith in the Lord and have grown in following Jesus Christ.

The great names of the Bible are those servants of God who were instruments through whom he brought blessings to the world; even Jesus himself was the Instrument, the One through whom God created all things (Colossians 1:16). The Hall of Fame of Faith chapter, Hebrews 11, is the chapter of great instruments of God: Abraham, Moses, David, Elijah, and the great servants of the Old Testament are those "who through faith conquered kingdoms, administered justice and gained what was promised; who shut the mouths of lions, quenched the fury of the flames, and escaped the edge of the sword; whose weakness was turned to strength;

and who became powerful in battle and routed foreign armies" (Hebrews 11:33-34).

GRACE

We start serving God by serving others the same way God starts with us—grace! That is, God's unmerited favor, undeserved mercy, and abundant blessings. Gary Sweeten was one of the great teachers on the staff of College Hill for many years. He developed many of the courses that brought people from around the globe to learn, and which in time spread to churches worldwide. One of his favorite phrases was, "It's all grace, folks, it's all grace."

Grace was first on the mind of the apostle Paul in writing about the things of God. He begins his letters in the New Testament with some version of "Grace and peace"—often together, but always grace. Paul used the word "grace" eighty times in his letters. According to Paul, we are saved by grace (Ephesians 2:5), are justified by grace (Romans 3:24), live under grace rather than law (Romans 6:14), and have spiritual gifts because of grace (Romans 12:6).

Before his conversion, Saul was a hard man; he was a member of a movement so concerned with strict observation of rules that it persecuted and killed Christians. But Paul was conscious of God's grace to him and was transformed in showing grace toward others. Early in his ministry Paul had a disagreement with Barnabas about the ministry of Mark (Acts 15:37-39). Yet at the end of his life, he is back in fellowship with Mark and reaches out to him for support. He writes to Timothy, "Only Luke is with me. Get Mark and bring him with you, because he is helpful to me in my ministry" (2 Timothy 4:11).

John Newton, the author of the hymn "Amazing Grace," knew about grace. Once the captain of slave ships, he knew he did not deserve God's grace. Yet he knew, too, that God's grace brought him to repentance and faith. Through his writing and influence on William Wilberforce, Newton was instrumental in the eventual abolishing of the slave trade in the British Empire.

As we pray for God to make us an instrument of his grace, we expect God to use us to benefit others. This takes work! Karen Lane was the founder of the ministry known as *Feast of Love* in Cincinnati. Like the apostle Paul and John Newton, she had a shameful past. But she was a tremendous instrument of God's grace—it came through in her actions. First she started serving a meal for hungry people in Cincinnati one Christmas. Then there was a meal for Easter, and then Thanksgiving. Then it wasn't just for one year, but every year. Then she began to minister to the shut-ins—taking food to those who couldn't come to the meal in the church fellowship hall. Then her vision grew to *Tools for Schools*—providing school supplies for children in the inner city. Then she began a weekend event for inner-city children to have an outdoor camping experience. Then she organized a number of schools to look for other ways to help the needy with her Find a Need and Fill It program. Thousands of people were touched through her ministries. She did not feel like a "gracious" person, but she was an instrument of God's grace. She knew God had graced her, and she knew that it was right that she should be an instrument of grace to others.

People around you, in your family, church, workplace, or neighborhood, may or may not deserve a helping hand. They may even be offensive.

But God knows that none of us deserves God's helping hand. He helps because he is gracious. In the same way, we pray that God would make us gracious people who look for ways to provide help, support, and care to others—because it is God's way, the way God has blessed us and what God calls us to do.

TRUTH

When we pray to be instruments of truth, we are asking God to make us standard bearers and trustworthy messengers to those who are trapped in the ultimate lie. But before we can be instruments for others, we have to know the truth ourselves.

If you were to ask me to name the greatest spiritual blessings in my life, memorizing the Word of God would be one of them. I began to memorize Scripture the week I met Christ. I was greatly helped in memorizing the Word through Dawson Trotman and the Navigators ministry. Dawson began his growth in the Lord as he wrote out verses he was memorizing on small cards that he would carry with him everywhere. Inspired by him, for years I have written Scripture on small cards that I carry with me and review regularly. The memorized Word has empowered and refreshed me again and again. Now, I confess that I have started and stopped many times throughout my life. But it is something I keep coming back to, because I know the strength it provides. I am presently memorizing more Scripture than any other time in my life.

If we are to be instruments of God's truth, it is not enough to know it. We must believe it. "To the Jews who had believed him, Jesus said, 'If you hold to my teaching, you are really my disciples. Then you will know the truth, and the truth will set you free'" (John 8:32-33). It is not just biblical knowledge that sets us free; it is *believing biblical truth*. Jesus is the same yesterday, today, and forever, but knowing this is not enough. It is believing this that is transforming. In 2 Corinthians 1:20 we read, "For no matter how many promises God has made, they are 'Yes' in Christ." When I memorized this verse; that was good. When I believed it; that was glorious!

I shared with you in a previous chapter that as a young pastor I struggled with feelings of inadequacy. I felt that the things I was doing were too big for me. It was when I believed God had a plan for my life, and that he could fulfill his plan, that I was set free from my feelings of inadequacy. Paul writes, "For we are God's workmanship, created in Christ Jesus to do good works, which God prepared in advance for us to do" (Ephesians 2:10). Through the prophet Jeremiah, God told his people, "'For I know the plans I have for you,' declares the LORD, 'plans to prosper you and not to harm you, plans to give you hope and a future'" (Jeremiah 29:11).

I don't believe that God's people have a very good understanding of the power of God's Word when we believe it! It is believing that has carried me into and through many challenges in my ministry. I could never have left College Hill at fifty-five to found pureHOPE if I had not believed that God was calling and that he had a destiny for me. It is because I have continued to believe that truth that I am now engaged in this ministry of the Prayer Covenant during this period of my life.

As I mentioned in a preceding chapter, one of the ways that I feel called to bring both grace and truth to people is to call them with spiritual encouragement. I almost never end a phone call without sharing Scripture and praying. Since I believe it is important to share God's truth, I seek to depend on the Lord, asking in my heart—what Scripture does God want to speak to that person? And then when I share a verse, it is amazing, because so often the person will say, "That's so good. It was just what I needed."

When we want to know the truth, we turn to Jesus Christ. Jesus is full of both grace and truth. "The Word became flesh and made his dwelling among us. We have seen his glory, the glory of the One and Only, who came from the Father, full of grace and truth" (John 1:14). Jesus embodies the beautiful balance between grace and truth. Some people emphasize all grace or all truth, but they need to go together. While grace embraces us in our failings like the forgiving hug of a loving parent, truth is firm, hard, unchanging, and reliable—like a diamond that reflects light. Truth is something that many in our modern world adjust to their own desires and lifestyle. They presume that what passes for truth is just personal opinion.

Jesus was very clear about the centrality and primacy of truth. He stands in total contradiction to untruth. Speaking of Satan, Jesus says, "He was a murderer from the beginning, not holding to the truth, for there is no truth in him. When he lies, he speaks his native language, for he is a liar and the father of lies" (John 8:44). The world fractured into shards of conflict, chaos, and death when Adam and Eve believed the lie and failed to trust the truth of the Word of God. Only as we embrace truth do we have any hope to escape the consequences of the Lie.

Jesus says that he is truth in the flesh: "I am the way and the truth and the life" (John 14:6). And he wants us to know that the Scriptures are truth in writing. In his final prayer for his disciples present and future Jesus prays, "Sanctify them by the truth; your word is truth" (John 17:17).

FORGIVENESS

Forgiveness is one of God's great blessings. King David says, "Blessed is he whose transgressions are forgiven, whose sins are covered. Blessed is the man whose sin the LORD does not count against him and in whose spirit is no deceit" (Psalm 32:1-2).

Forgiveness has several layers. First, we must receive forgiveness. Just as we must believe the truth of God's Word, we must believe it for our own forgiveness. Once we have received the forgiveness of God, we pass it on. As we are filled with the forgiveness of God, we are unleashed to serve him in forgiving others. Grace, truth, and forgiveness have very deep relationships with one another. In the Lord's Prayer we are to pray, "Forgive us our debts as we also have forgiven our debtors" (Matthew 6:12). Forgiving others is not easy. I have a relationship that I am working on right now that is not yet resolved. To forgive is tough!

Not to forgive, however, is even tougher. One of the greatest stories in the Bible is about the forgiveness of Joseph toward his brothers. Sold into slavery in Egypt by his brothers, Joseph had good reason to be angry, and it was going to be tough for him to forgive. But he did. As the prime minister of Egypt, Joseph was in perfect position to get revenge when his brothers came looking for food to deal with the famine in their country. However, he forgives them instead.

Then Joseph said to his brothers, "Come close to me." When they had done so, he said, "I am your brother Joseph, the one you sold into Egypt! And now, do not be distressed and do not be angry with yourselves for selling me here, because it was to save lives that God sent me ahead of you. For two years now there has been famine in the land, and for the next five years there will not be plowing and reaping. But God sent me ahead of you to preserve for you a remnant on earth and to save your lives by a great deliverance." (Genesis 45:4-7)

I was an adjunct professor at Fuller Theological Seminary in Pasadena, California, for three years. One time I took my twenty-two-year-old son, Timothy, with me. I planned for him to see the Rose Bowl football game, to be in my class, and even help me teach the class. It was a great trip. During the class, when we got to the part about family life, I invited Timothy to join in. I said to Tim, "I am going to ask you to leave the class while I teach about family life and talk about our family; you won't hear what I say. Then you come in and teach about our family while I will leave. I won't hear what you say. Then I will come back in and we can answer questions together."

"That sounds like fun!" he said.

When we got back together, the interaction with the students was powerful. In fact, it was one of the most dynamic teaching situations I have ever been a part of. When the class ended, a student asked, "Would you two have lunch with me and a few others from my congregation?" While we were eating, one of those who came with the student turned to Timothy and sternly asked, "Is your dad the same at home as he is at church?"

"Yes," Timothy said. "Dad is a sinner at home and a sinner at church. But we forgive him at home, and they forgive him at church."

As you may have guessed, the angry visitor was the son of a pastor. In his family there was hypocrisy at home and hypocrisy at church. And there was anger at home and anger at the church. No forgiveness anywhere. It is forgiveness that cuts through these knots and overcomes our divisions and our failings. Forgiveness is so important in our families, our congregations, and our communities. Richard Halverson, the former pastor of Fourth Presbyterian Church in Washington, D.C., and later the chaplain of the Senate, used to say that unforgiveness shatters relationships and forgiveness heals them.

Forgiveness brings health to our relationships and our souls. David Seamands, who passed away in 2006, had a powerful ministry of pastoral counseling. Once, when he was visiting someone in a mental institution, he spoke with one of the counseling staff. The counselor remarked to him as they walked toward the parking lot after his visit, "Half the people here could leave this afternoon if they could believe that they were forgiven." When I read that comment, thinking of the Lord's Prayer, I said to myself, "Yes, and most of the other half could leave if they would forgive!" How much of what happens in counselors' offices around the country is about forgiveness of past hurts, and relationships that have been buried and fester with painful emotions and unhealthy thoughts?

I have seen the power of being God's instrument of forgiveness by asking for forgiveness both within my family and my pastorate. One time my parents were coming to visit, and I knew they would be arriving at the airport within two hours. I worked at the church until the last minute and then came home to get my family to drive with me to the airport. My two youngest children—Stephen and Kristy—came to me, excited to tell me about their day. I paid attention to Stephen first and then to Kristy. Kristy didn't like being second and threw a tantrum. "You don't take me seriously. You paid attention to him first!"

Then I threw a tantrum; I spanked her—hard. Another of my daughters, Kari, saw me spank her sister and ran out of the room, crying and saying, "I can't stand to see my daddy beat up on my little sister."

In the midst of this swirl of family tantrums, I was wondering how to pull things together in order to pick up my parents from the airport with a good spirit.

So, step by step, I started to address our issues. "Kristy, could I talk with you?" We sat on the couch in the family room. I apologized. I said, "Honey, I spanked you too hard for the small thing that you did. Will you forgive me?"

"Oh yes, Daddy. I forgive you. I knew you were going to ask for my forgiveness." We hugged and prayed. I thanked God for her gracious spirit. Then I thought to myself—what do I do to get back with Kari? I came to the bottom of the steps and called to her. She came down slowly.

"Honey, you were right, I did spank your sister too hard. She didn't deserve that. I have asked for her forgiveness, and she has forgiven me. I didn't think I was beating up on her. I was spanking her. My pride was hurt deeply by what you said. I am truly sorry that I spanked her so hard. And I am sorry that I wounded your spirit by doing so. Will you forgive me?" She hesitated but said yes. With that I loaded up the car to get Mom and Dad.

As I thought about it, there was real healing with Kristy. But with Kari, I sensed that this was only the first step. I did not want a root of bitterness to grow. Later, we got alone and we had a chance to talk at length. Again, I asked for her forgiveness. This time it was real. I praise God that she did forgive me. That root could have grown and built a barrier between us.

RIGHTEOUSNESS

The second set of life verses for me, as I mentioned in an earlier chapter, was John 17:17-19. In his high priestly prayer Jesus prays to the Father, "Sanctify them by the truth; your word is truth. As you sent me into the world, I have sent them into the world. For them I sanctify myself, that they too may be truly sanctified." Jesus says he sanctified himself for the sake of the disciples. Then he says that he sanctified himself for the sake of those who will believe through the disciples' word, which includes all of us. In this prayer Jesus is praying that his followers—all those who comprise his church—would "hunger and thirst for righteousness" (Matthew 5:6) just the way he does.

I began to think and pray those verses as God placed on my heart a concern for the loss of sexual purity that was increasing around our country. This is not what God wants; it grieves him. Paul writes to the Christians at Ephesus, "But among you there must not be even a hint of sexual immorality, or of any kind of impurity, or of greed, because these are improper for God's holy people" (Ephesians 5:3).

If we are to live righteous and holy lives, then we have to step away from unrighteous and unholy actions. In biblical terms, that means that we sanctify/consecrate ourselves as Jesus did. It was for our sake that he consecrated himself! He was serving us; he had us in mind as he lived his righteous life. Inspired by Jesus, I asked myself, "For whose sake do I consecrate myself? Who do I care for enough that I will be careful to guard my behavior and my thought life?"

I want to be sure that my life does not destroy the lives of others because of a bad example. Our personal choices are never just about "me." We are connected to so many others, and how we behave and think affects them. To be an instrument of righteousness is to be concerned with how my moral behavior affects all those around me. How can a Christian man consider undermining the honor of Christ and destroying the moral strength of his family by flirting with and following sexual sin—and then seeing the devastation he has wrought?

First John 3:1-3 became the foundational passage for pureHOPE.

> How great is the love the Father has lavished on us, that we should be called children of God! And that is what we are! The reason the world does not know us is that it did not know him. Dear friends, now we are children of God, and what we will be has not yet been made known. But we know that when he appears, we shall be like him, for we shall see him as he is. Everyone who has this hope in him purifies himself, just as he is pure. (1 John 3:1-3)

As I was traveling around the country to encourage pastors to teach and preach on sexual purity, I was privileged to meet with Adrian Rodgers in a hotel lobby in Jacksonville, Florida. He was on the executive committee of the *Religious Alliance Against Pornography*, pastor of Belleview Baptist Church, and the president of the Southern Baptist Convention. He was a dear brother in Christ with a significant leadership role. He sat next to President Reagan when the *Religious Alliance Against Pornography* met with the president and Attorney General Edwin Meese seeking stronger legislation against obscenity. Their efforts, along with those of others, led to the strongest legislation against pornography in our nation's history.

After we met in the hotel lobby, Rodgers invited me upstairs to a meeting of the speakers for a conference of Southern Baptist pastors and leaders, saying, "I want them to meet you." When we entered the room, Adrian's presence was so significant that all conversation ceased. He said to the group, "I want you to meet my friend Jerry. Tell them why you are here."

I shared briefly and thanked them for the privilege of attending the conference. A few minutes later one of the speakers came to me and said, "You don't have to tell me how important this battle against pornography is, because my heart has been broken. My best friend from seminary, pastor of a rapidly growing church, just recently confessed to consuming pornography and having an affair. He had to resign from his pulpit, his family is wounded, and his life is broken." And then he went on, "I also know it is important because a young man came to me four months ago—lead singer of a great Christian group—told me of his addiction to pornography. He came to me and pleaded with me, 'Pastor, you must help me. I cannot live with this. It is destroying my life.' He was the father of four children. I tried to help him and thought I had, but I failed. Two weeks ago he killed himself. We need to do more. Thank you for what you are doing."

I began this ministry against pornography and to encourage sexual purity because such unrighteous behavior seduces, exploits and consumes, and then it enslaves and destroys. Because of the

Internet the problem is a million times worse than when I started in the battle in the 1980s. If Christian men are to be instruments of righteousness, then we need to be in accountability groups or at least have an accountability partner. *Covenant Eyes* (**www. covenanteyes.com**) is an excellent internet program that allows two or more people who desire to live a pure life to know every website visited by the other as a way of holding each other accountable. It is a great resource for helping men who want to be delivered from their issues with pornography. For the sake of the young people of this nation, Christians need to lead by example and give themselves to righteousness, holding one another accountable to sexual purity.

JUSTICE

Righteousness is the right-hand partner of justice. God is the God of righteousness and justice. "The LORD loves righteousness and justice; the earth is full of his unfailing love" (Psalm 33:5). And in Psalm 89:14 we read, "Righteousness and justice are the foundation of your throne; love and faithfulness go before you."

The Old Testament prophets were concerned for justice, as the prophet Amos called out, "But let justice roll on like a river, righteousness like a never-failing stream!" (Amos 5:24). And of course Jesus is concerned with justice. He says "Woe to you Pharisees, because you give God a tenth of your mint, rue and all other kinds of garden herbs, but you neglect justice and the love of God. You should have practiced the latter without leaving the former undone" (Luke 11:42).

We need to care about justice as much as we care about

righteousness. Pornography is both a righteousness issue and a justice issue. Every time a man looks at pornography he is financing the sex industry. He fuels the sex industry that produces sex trafficking, enslaving so many of our teenagers in America and around the world. How is it possible that Christian men don't run from it? We have to care about justice—the value of persons and young people. Matthew 18:14 emphasizes the value of the one lost sheep: " . . . your Father in heaven is not willing that any of these little ones should perish."

Do we believe that Jesus knew what he was talking about? Do we believe that Jesus was right? Do we know that the young people of America are being destroyed by moral ambiguity and promiscuity, which has led to epidemics of sexually transmitted diseases, before they know the wonder and beauty of God's plan? This is an issue of righteousness and justice.

We need to care and pray about racial justice, joblessness, and the poor as much as we care about righteousness! I am part of a group in Cincinnati called the City Servants. About two-fifths are African American pastors. Through them we have been made aware of the unique challenges African Americans face growing up in our culture. The other day when we were meeting, one of my white brothers said to our African American brothers and sisters, "It's all about economics, isn't it?" The spontaneous response of all them was, "Yes, it is!"

These are successful leaders, and they have faced racial issues all their lives—pastoring people at every level of the economic ladder. Most of them have dealt with economic issues throughout their lives as well. They know that they have to be better—not just equivalent—at what they do in order to be hired over a Caucasian person. I know there are exceptions to this, but this has been their experience. They face challenges in the workplace and in our culture that most whites have never experienced or understood.

When I think about this, I move into compassion mode—it breaks my heart; but I still haven't addressed the problem! I must feel compassion and I must act. My studies in Søren Kierkegaard challenge me here. He wrote, "Speak the truth consistent with the truth. Do the truth with passion." The work of justice is hard. I have to keep at it and stay focused. There is much that I have to learn and more that I need to do. More than I want to admit, I move on to new truths before I have lived the first truth that I have been shown.

CONCLUSION

We want God to use us; we want to be his instrument—there is no greater privilege. This request is a big one: "Make me an instrument of your grace, truth, forgiveness, righteousness, and justice." In this prayer request we are praying, "Let your will be done; let your kingdom come, as in heaven, also on the earth." Only we are also praying, "Let it come in me and through me." For God to answer this prayer, we have to be ready to grow and change. We are not asking for behavior modification but for transformed hearts and transformed lives!

REFLECTION QUESTIONS

Chapter 9   Influence

1. We want God to use us and to make the world a better place. How can praying the Prayer Covenant help you participate with God in doing just that?

2. Ministry, channel, agent and instrument are words that we use to talk about ways that God works through us. From your reading of this chapter, why do I prefer the word instrument? Which do you prefer?

3. As a young Christian I was delighted to discover that God used prayers that I prayed with my friend Si to obtain Frontier Ranch for Young Life in Colorado. It truly is good when God uses us. How is God using you to bless others?

4. Grace, truth, forgiveness, righteousness and justice are essential ways God works through his people. Which of these do you most naturally express and which are you inclined to ignore? How does each contribute to transforming the world around you?

5. This chapter closes by referring to the Lord's Prayer. What parallels can you discover between the Lord's Prayer and the Prayer Covenant? How do these parallels provide insight on prayer?

CHAPTER 10
DISCIPLESHIP

THE NEXT STEP IN THE Prayer Covenant is moving from influence to discipleship. God wants us to be disciples of Jesus Christ, and he wants to use us to disciple others. When we pray, "Use me today for your glory, and to invite others to follow Jesus Christ as Lord," we are allowing God to disciple us through praying the Prayer Covenant, and God is using us to disciple others through sharing the prayer. There are four key ideas in this request: that God would "use me," that he would use me "for his glory," that he would use me "today," and that he would use me to "invite others."

USE ME

When we pray "use me," this is another way to pray that God would make each of us an "instrument," the request we explored in the previous chapter. But there is more to be said. When we pray "use me," we are signing up, making ourselves available to God—to be disciples. Because we are disciples, we don't want to be sitting in the stands; we want to be on the team, in the game, on the field, doing our part. Our prayer for God to "use me" is intimately connected to our praying the prayer of commitment, "Jesus, be Lord of my life." We are also making the request of dependence, "Fill me with your Holy Spirit," as we seek spiritual power to serve his purposes and bear much fruit.

When Jesus called the first disciples he told them up front that he had a purpose for them. "'Come, follow me,' Jesus said, 'and I will make you fishers of men'" (Mark 1:17). How God uses us will vary from person to person and be shaped by our gifts, abilities, relationships, and backgrounds. More often than not we will be surprised. And it will mean that God must change us, shape us, and transform us. That is his plan.

A pastor friend of mine met the Lord as a college student. As a boy he had attended church but renounced his faith as a young teenager when there was conflict, sickness, and death in his family. In his first year of college, the Lord called him into faith and out of his anger and unbelief. In those early months after his conversion, he used to lay awake at night afraid that God was going to call him to be a pastor—the last thing in the world he wanted to be, even as a believer. After college he went to seminary, not to be a pastor, he said, but because he wanted to know more about God. Then after seminary he returned to the college campus as a staff member with a campus ministry. He loved starting Bible studies and building campus fellowship groups that bore witness to Christ and encouraged rigorous discipleship. After a few years he grew frustrated, because just as he would develop good leaders and a spiritually vital group, the leaders graduated. One day he was musing on how wonderful it would be to be able to have a community of believers who weren't always graduating and moving away. Then it dawned on him that what he wanted was the church—a community of believers who were growing in the Lord and were in one place for more than just four years. At that point he became a pastor. Now he can't believe it took him fifteen years to get there!

Many of us will have our fears and misconceptions about being used by God. But God knows what he is doing. What he has in mind for you is better than what you have in mind for yourself. When we ask God to "use me" we are inviting him to get past our fears, barriers, and inhibitions. How is God working in you to make you what he wants you to be and to place you where he can use you best?

I never expected that I would devote so much of my life to fighting pornography and the sexual addictions of our world today. Growing up, I wanted to be a professional tennis player. Then I wanted to be a youth leader. Finally I wanted to be a pastor. Who could know that I would leave the congregation and ministry I loved so deeply to confront the sexualizing of America through pornography, sexual exploitation, and sex trafficking?

The point of asking God to use us is that it takes us beyond ourselves to bigger purposes. It was believing that Jesus was Lord and that his plan (the Father's plan) is to unite all things in Christ— "to bring all things in heaven and on earth together under one head" (Ephesians 1:10)—that led me to believe that God could bring good out of evil. He could use the scourge of pornography, the rape of women, and the molestation of children to drive his people to their knees and to each other. I received courage from this conviction that God could use even me to call various Christian denominational leaders in our country, as well as Mormon, Jewish, and Muslim leaders, to come together to fight this scourge as well.

We can believe God can "use me" because Jesus tells us that he wants us to bear much fruit. "This is to my Father's glory, that you bear much fruit, showing yourselves to be my disciples" (John 15:8). And the disciples and his church have borne great fruit through the centuries! Remember, he sent us out, saying, "Therefore go and make disciples of all nations . . . teaching them to obey everything I have commanded you" (Matthew 28:19-20). This is Jesus' call to be in partnership with the sovereign Lord of the universe. God plans to use you!

This Great Commission of Jesus was not just for the apostles or for those called to professional ministry. He commissions all of us in his kingdom, and he expects us to use the abilities and resources he has given us. This is clear from the parable of the talents in Matthew 25. "Again, it will be like a man going on a journey, who called his servants and entrusted his property to them. To one he gave five talents of money, to another two talents, and to another one talent, each according to his ability" (Matthew 25:14-15). The master commended the two who used their talents; he rebuked the one who buried his one talent:

> Then the man who had received the one talent came. "Master," he said, "I knew that you are a hard man, harvesting where you have not sown and gathering where you have not scattered seed. So I was afraid and went out and hid your talent in the ground. See, here is what belongs to you."

> His master replied, "You wicked, lazy servant! So you knew that I harvest where I have not sown and gather where I have not scattered seed? Well then, you should have put my money on deposit with the bankers, so that when I returned I would have received it back with interest." (Matthew 25:24-27)

God has given each of us gifts, abilities, and talents, and he wants us to use them. During seminary I wrestled with the issue of purity of motivation in wanting to bear much fruit. It was a real struggle. Does humility mean that I should not seek to do great things for God? How much was my desire to make an impact for Christ just an expression of my pride? I realized that if I tried to do nothing that my motivations were mixed; and if I tried to "go for it" my motivations were mixed. So I decided that I would go for it and acknowledge to the Lord and myself that my motives are not pure.

So I leave it to him to sort out my heart and to purify my motivation. In the meantime I wanted God to use me, wherever and however he pleases.

As we ask God to use us, we must keep in mind that bearing fruit for God is not the same thing as our idea of success and producing huge results that impress. Frankly, we are not called to be fruit inspectors. We must not only leave the motives of our heart up to God but also the results.

THE BATTLE OF DISCIPLESHIP

As we pray for God to use us for his glory, we must keep in mind that we are engaged in a battle. The apostle Paul knew what he was talking about from personal experience when he wrote, "For our struggle is not against flesh and blood, but against the rulers, against the authorities, against the powers of this dark world and against the spiritual forces of evil in the heavenly realms" (Ephesians 6:12).

As my ministry of fighting pornography grew and I considered leaving my congregation and working full time to lead pureHOPE, it became clear to me that part of what we were doing was confronting the Mafia, because they controlled so much of the production and distribution of hardcore pornography. One day when Patty was shopping I felt great danger. I was alone in the house; I closed and locked the doors and looked to see if anyone might be able to see in the windows. I experienced real terror for the first time in my life. That is the only way to describe it. In facing that fear, I found comfort and peace in the Scriptures, particularly Hebrews 12:2:

"Let us fix our eyes on Jesus, the author and perfecter of our faith, who for the joy set before him endured the cross, scorning its shame, and sat down at the right hand of the throne of God." When I remembered that Jesus is Lord at the right hand of God, I knew that if Jesus wanted me to be safe, then I was as safe confronting members of the Mafia as I would be in continuing to pastor College Hill.

Then I went on to memorize the verses that followed: "Consider him who endured such opposition from sinners, so that you will not grow weary and lose heart. In your struggle against sin, you have not yet resisted to the point of shedding your blood" (Hebrews 12: 3-4). I'm sure glad I didn't memorize these verses before I had learned again that Jesus is on the throne. The peace of God settled in my heart as I knew I was safe within his purposes. I have that peace this day.

It is not easy to serve God's glory—not only does it cut against our personal self-centeredness and the spirit of the age, it also means that we are opposed by forces of spiritual darkness. This means conflict, struggle, and suffering. Jesus is our model—his commitment to God's glory took him to the Garden of Gethsemane and then to the cross. Each of the apostles encountered persecution, imprisonment, and death. Your battles for the glory of God may not be so dramatic, but they will be just as real.

Mother Teresa was one of God's great leaders, so focused on the glory of God. I sense this in her writing; I sensed it when I had the privilege of speaking with her on the phone. She was to be the keynote speaker for the *Religious Alliance Against Pornography* conference in Washington, D.C. There 430 leaders from politics, business, and clergy were coming from across the country. Two weeks before the conference, her doctor would not let her travel for health reasons. I called her to get ideas she had planned to share so I could deliver some of her thoughts. This was intimidating. I didn't feel good representing her! She assured me that on the day she was to speak, "I and my 250 novitiates will spend the entire day in prayer so that God will give you much grace." That was very humbling and reassuring.

So I asked her, "What can we pray for you?" She responded spontaneously, "That I not spoil God's work." She wanted to be used for God's glory. She didn't want to be in the way. Her response was even more humbling. Today I don't remember what she told me about pornography. What I remember is her passion for God's glory and the needs of people.

In an interesting side note: several years later I was on a plane traveling to Los Angeles and was bumped from my assigned seat and taken up to a vacant seat in first class. I struck up a conversation with the woman in the seat beside me. She said she was returning from the funeral of Mother Teresa. She said, "I was her physician."

"Really?" I said. "Did you know that she was going to speak at our Religious Alliance Conference several years ago but had to cancel for medical reasons?"

She said, "I am the doctor who told her she could not travel."

You, nor I, will ever be a Mother Teresa, but when we seek to be used for God's glory we are important. In God's plan and purposes there are no little people and no unimportant tasks.

TODAY

"Today" is an underlying theme throughout the Prayer Covenant. We want Jesus to be Lord of our lives *today*..." Someday, in Christ, we will see God's glory unveiled. One day every knee will bow and every tongue confess that Jesus is Lord (Philippians 2:10-11). One day "every eye will see him" (Revelation 1:7). Every believer lives for that day. We are waiting for it, hoping for it and living for it. "When Christ, who is your life, appears, then you also will appear with him in glory" (Colossians 3:4).

When we read the Bible, we may be tempted to look back on those Bible times as the real times of God's glory. How amazing it must have been to walk through the Red Sea and see God showing his power in such a dramatic way. We wonder what it might have been like to be with the disciples in the boat when Jesus rebuked the waves and calmed the storm. "Who is this? Even the wind and the waves obey him!" (Mark 4:41).

It is right that we look forward with anticipation to what God will do and to look back with appreciation at the accounts of what God has done. But God has placed us in this time and place, and it is for "today" that we want to be used for God's glory. Jesus proclaimed, "The kingdom of God is near" (Mark 1:15). The Greek word translated "is near" means "right now" and "in this place."

There is spiritual warfare going on to keep you from serving God today. C. S. Lewis shines light on this dimension of the spiritual battle in his fictional correspondence *The Screwtape Letters*, a part of which we examined in an earlier chapter. Screwtape, the senior tempter, regards God as the enemy and guides the junior tempter Wormwood on how to hinder his "patient":

> The humans live in time but our Enemy destines them to eternity. ... He would therefore have them continually concerned either with eternity... or with the Present—either meditating on their eternal union with, or separation from, Himself, or else obeying the present voice of conscience, bearing the present cross, receiving the present grace, giving thanks for the present pleasure.
>
> Our business is to get them away from the eternal, and from the Present.[21]

When we get trapped in the past, our thoughts keep going back to previous pains and struggles of which we can't let go. Consciously and subconsciously, we are not living for today. When we live for today in the Lord, we let go of those past hurts. We give them to the Lord and become free to live in the present. When we get trapped in the future, we become filled with anxieties about what might happen. We may become paralyzed or obsessively preoccupied. Perhaps you have heard the old saying, "I have faced many fears and dangers, most of which never happened"? When we let go of future fears, all that emotional energy spent in anxiety is unleashed into the present. That is surely why Jesus said, "Therefore do not worry about tomorrow, for tomorrow will worry about itself. Each day has enough trouble of its own" (Matthew 6:34).

While in college, after I had been a Christian for about three years, it dawned on me that I was inclined to be a "people pleaser." I was struck by Paul's words, "Am I now trying to win the approval of human beings, or of God? Or am I trying to please people? If I were still trying to please people, I would not be a servant of Christ"

---

21 (The Screwtape Letters [San Francisco: HarperSanFrancisco, 2002], p. 155).

(Galatians 1:10). Since that realization, I find myself frequently asking, "What motivates me?" I want my motivation to be right, because I want to please the Lord, today.

Living for the Lord today is a mindset. It's about the attitude by which we go through each day. Am I living this day for myself or am I living for God? When your supervisor at work fails to give you credit for something you have achieved, and worse, takes credit for your work, will you allow anger and resentment to possess you, or will you recall that you weren't really working for your boss anyway? When your family takes you for granted in the give and take of life together, will you hold it against them, or will you let it go because you were really serving the Lord in those chores? God is glorified when we handle these humbling situations with grace because we are conscious of him.

When God becomes our motivation, we are empowered to do great things. Mother Teresa said it this way:

> People are often unreasonable, illogical and self-centered; forgive them anyway.
> If you are kind, people may accuse you of selfish, ulterior motives; be kind anyway.
> If you are successful, you will win some false friends and some true enemies; succeed anyway.
> If you are honest and frank, people may cheat you; be honest and frank anyway.
> What you spend years building, someone could destroy overnight; build anyway.
> If you find serenity and happiness, they may be jealous; be happy anyway.

The good you do today, people will often forget tomorrow;
do good anyway.
Give the world the best you have, and it may never be
enough; give the world the best you've got anyway.
You see, in the final analysis, it is between you and your God;
it was never between you and them anyway.[22]

The question we must face as we wake each morning is this: "How does God want to use me for this day?"

Eternal God,

our beginning and our end,

be our starting point and our haven,

and accompany us in this day's journey.

Use our hands

to do the work of your creation,

and use our lives

to bring others the new life you give this world

in Jesus Christ, Redeemer of all.[23]

How precious "this day" is. Today is not business as usual. It is the day the Lord has given us, and we cannot know how limited our time here on earth is. We don't want to waste time. We are not looking for past times to cope with aimlessness and boredom. We want to make the most of each day for eternal purposes. We want our lives to count. Whatever God is going to do, what he does in us and through us today, is what best prepares us for what he will

---

22 (Lucinda Vardey, *Mother Teresa: A Simple Path* [New York: Ballantine Books, 1995], p. 185).
23 ("Daily Prayer," Book of Common Worship [Louisville: Westminster John Knox Press, 1993], p. 37)

do in us and through us for tomorrow and on into eternity. We live with the perspective Jesus wants us to have as he taught us to pray, "Give us today our daily bread" (Matthew 6:11). We want to live with the same perspective as King David, who wrote, "This is the day that the LORD has made; let us rejoice and be glad in it" (Psalm 118:24).

INVITING OTHERS

That morning prayer I just quoted asks God to use us "to bring others the new life you give this world in Jesus Christ, Redeemer of all." If we know Jesus, there is an inner desire to want others to know him as well. That is why we pray in our Prayer Covenant, "Use me today for your glory and to invite others to follow Jesus Christ as Lord." We want to tell the story. We want to get the good news out. Looking at churches through the years, we can see that there is something about Christianity that is incurably evangelistic. Inviting others to Jesus is part of our DNA.

In his book *Crazy Love*, Francis Chan writes about a fourteen-year-old girl, Brooke Bronkowski, who lived each day with the love of God in her heart and a desire to invite others to follow Jesus Christ. During her freshman year in high school Brooke was killed in a car accident. Nearly fifteen hundred people came to her memorial service. In one sense, you could say that her death was a tragedy; but that is only if you failed to look at her life in light of eternity and the glory of God. In her journal Brooke wrote, "I'll live my life to the fullest. I'll brighten up... I will loosen up. I will tell others about Christ... I will give others the joy I have and God will give me more joy. I will do everything God tells me to do. I will follow the footsteps of God. I will do my best!!!!"[24]

Francis Chan shared the gospel at her memorial service and reports that at least two hundred students expressed a desire to confess Jesus Christ as Lord and knelt at the front of the sanctuary. Brooke kept Bibles in her garage, hoping to give them to her unchurched friends, and the ushers at the service passed them out to all who came forward. No doubt, Brooke now in heaven, is delighted that God used her for his glory.

Asking God to use us to invite others into his kingdom is so important for our day, for today. One Sunday morning a pastor was preparing for service and lamented to God that attendance had been dropping. "What should we do?" he asked the Lord. He didn't hear a voice, but in those ways that God speaks to his people he heard a simple answer. "Invite them!"

We live in a society awash in spiritual darkness. The tides of unbelief are flooding our world. The rise of our sexualized culture is just one manifestation. Another is the chaos and greed that infects our economy. You can probably think of a lot of other ways unbelief is affecting us. But we need not be discouraged. We need to pray. This is not the first time the floods of unbelief have risen so high. It has happened before. But there were those who cried out to God. The Haystack Prayer Meeting, held in Williamstown, Massachusetts, in August 1806, unleashed a movement of inviters that affected the entire world for generations. During a thunderstorm, five students took refuge in a haystack and prayed. Within four years they began recruiting friends to go to the mission field. During the nineteenth

---

24 (Francis Chan, *Crazy Love* [Colorado Springs: David C. Cook, 2013], p. 48).

century, the work they initiated resulted in sending missionaries to China, Hawaii, and other nations in southeast Asia, winning many to Christ and establishing hospitals and schools.

In 1857 Jeremiah Lanphier called a noontime prayer meeting on Fulton Street in New York City because he was concerned about the spiritual state of the country. Six people came. The next week there were more. In six months there were ten thousand people in noonday prayer meetings in New York City. The fruit of those prayers multiplied. Estimates are that between 500,000 and a million people joined the church over the next several years because of the spiritual power unleashed through those prayer meetings.

We too can make an impact. It begins with prayer. A few years ago a group of ten or twelve college students who lived in Florida gathered one evening on a remote portion of the beach to pray. The moon was shining on the water; there was a gentle breeze, and the soft sounds of waves were breaking on the shore. Most students in the prayer meeting had their heads bowed. However, one student looked up just as two curious people walked up to the group. "What are you doing?" asked the two puzzled visitors.

"We're praying," was the answer. "Would you like to join us?"

So the two sat down and joined in. After the prayer time was over, the two visitors described how they had been attracted to the quiet little huddle of pray-ers—they felt as if they had been pulled over for some reason, though they couldn't say why. And after experiencing the presence of God in prayer, they were responsive to the lordship of Jesus Christ. That group grew, too. At the beginning of the summer there were fifteen students; at the end there were 150 students.

Who might God want to touch and lead through you? I have the multiplication principle of 2 Timothy 2:2 in view here: "And the things you have heard me say in the presence of many witnesses entrust to reliable people who will also be qualified to teach others." There are four generations of belief evident here: 1) Jesus Christ to Paul, 2) Paul to Timothy, 3) Timothy to reliable people, and 4) those who will be taught by the reliable people.

Building on the pattern of this multiplication principle, consider: who is discipling you? Who are you discipling? Who might those you disciple influence? I know that my life has been enriched and changed because, over forty-five years in ministry, I have joined in over nine thousand Prayer Covenants. I have known the power of their prayers, and I have been thrilled to hear story after story of how God has worked in the lives of people for whom I have been privileged to pray.

It is the vision of exalting Christ through praying and spreading the Prayer Covenant that led to writing this book. I invite you to join me in thinking beyond your immediate circle. How might this country be changed if hundreds of thousands or even millions of people were believing God and following Jesus with passion?

When I first began to invite others into the Prayer Covenant I wondered "Might God raise up a hundred men and a hundred women who would follow Jesus together in believing God and asking him to raise up a thousand men and women through their sharing this prayer? Might God use those thousand men and women to pray up ten thousand men and women, or even a hundred thousand men and women, who will grow in their passion for our Lord himself and the kingdom of God throughout the United States and the world?"

What I have discovered, is that it isn't actually working that way. That was too formal and structured. The way it is unfolding is that of one person touching another person. It is as two or three people or small groups of believers here and there are "following Jesus together." There are expanding circles as many sense that God is calling them to pray and share this prayer. It is spreading from person to person and from congregation to congregation. It is spreading city to city, from denomination to denomination and from country to country. This process has already begun.

God is causing this vision to grow. There are denominational leaders and pastors, para-church organizations and other strong leaders who share a passion for revival and awakening of the body of Christ throughout America and the world. God is powerfully at work and I am delighted that the Prayer Covenant is privileged to join with them as one more catalyst.

You are not reading this book by accident. Who are the people with whom you want to share this prayer and this book? Are we desperate enough for God and his glory, and for the spiritual impact of God's church, and its moral influence on our nation and the world, that we will make significant sacrifices of time and resources necessary for God's purposes?

God has already raised up hundreds and even thousands who are praying daily "Jesus be Lord of my life today in new ways." How long do you think it will take to inspire a million people to join the team?

If you are going to be an inviter, first pray this prayer for a week or two before you invite others to pray with you. Become comfortable with the prayer. Pay attention to how God is using it to change you. Once you get in touch with some of the ways that God is moving in your life, then you are ready to share your story with others and to invite them to join you in this movement of God. You might find it helpful to share a copy of this book with them so that they can gain a sense of how the Prayer Covenant got started and where it is going.

Once you are praying the Prayer Covenant with several people, make a point to listen to their story and hear how God is working in their lives. Give them a call or meet them for coffee. We are on a journey toward a future eternity. What matters is what Jesus Christ is doing in their lives—ten days from now, two months from now, six months from now, two years from now, ten years from now, and into forever. Listen to them, affirm them, and assure them of your prayers. And then, invite them to invite others. Give them a vision of how God can use them to raise up others who will in turn invite others into this great adventure of following Jesus as Lord together. Those who invite others will be among those who continue to pray the prayer six months later and six years later. Maybe even forty-five years later.

Of course, the goal is not really to get people to pray the Prayer Covenant. The goal is to "follow Jesus together" for the rest of our lives. The reason we begin with the Prayer Covenant is because it is intended to provide a taste of how sweet it is to know and follow Jesus together with fellow believers. As you follow Jesus together in prayer, you will find hope, spiritual insight, and power rising between you.

REFLECTION QUESTIONS

Chapter 10   Discipleship

1. As a young man I wanted to be a tennis player and became a pastor before I felt called to challenge the pornography industry. How has the hand of God shaped, and perhaps, surprised you?

2. What gifts, talents and abilities has God given you to be used for his glory? (Take some time with this penetrating challenge.) How do you rate your stewardship of these blessings from God?

3. How can focusing on *today* enrich your spiritual growth? Why is it that Satan wants us to live in the past or the future rather than focus on today?

4. How does Mother Teresa's meditation "*Anyway*" help you put discipleship into a practical perspective?

5. An essential element of discipleship is inviting others to follow Jesus. How can the Prayer Covenant be a helpful tool?

CHAPTER 11
AUTHORITY

THE FINAL LINE OF THE Prayer Covenant is not a request but an affirmation—well, perhaps more than an affirmation; it's a declaration: "I pray in the name of Jesus. Amen."

This is a common phrase, and many of us use it to end our prayers, but do we know what we are saying when we pray this? It is important that we pay attention to this line about praying in Jesus' name, because it is the only reason why any of our prayers are answered. It is, so to speak, the "send" button on our email. We may have typed a note to a friend, but our note won't get there if we don't click the "send" button or hit the "enter" key. Praying in Jesus' name affirms the basic attitude and way we pray from beginning to end. We pray in Jesus' authority, Jesus' character, and Jesus' will.

There are five affirmations when we say "in the name of Jesus, Amen." We are affirming our identity, our authority, our faith, our intentions, and our sincerity. We will consider each of these. Let's begin with our identity.

IDENTITY

God is our loving Creator who is eager to answer our prayers, but the teaching of the Bible from the Old Testament to the New is "not so fast" when it comes to getting our prayers answered. Prayer is a powerful mystery. When we make a prayer request, more than likely we are asking God to make something happen, to change something in the world. We need to pause and think about this. When a prayer is answered, the world, for all time, in some small or big way, is different from what it would have been if you had not prayed. Your prayers are literally world changing, whether they are big prayers or little prayers.

There are those who have a much smaller view of prayer in our modern world, if they pray at all. Writer L. T. C. Rolt said:

> I am not prepared to say that prayers of individuals can be separately and individually granted, that this would seem to be incompatible with the regular movements and the mechanism of the Universe, and it would seem impossible to explain why prayer should now be granted, now refused; but this I can assure you, that I have ever, in my difficulties, prayed fervently, and that—in the end—my prayers have been or have appeared to be granted, and I have received great comfort.[25]

This is not a biblical view of prayer at all! Even so, there are sincere believers who prefer to think of prayer as primarily meditation or conforming our desires to God's purposes. Prayer certainly includes meditation and surrender to God's will, but prayer is more than these. The Bible clearly records that things can change when we pray. The Red Sea opened because Moses prayed (Exodus 14:16). The sun stood still for Joshua in the battle with Israel's foes because Joshua prayed (Joshua 10:12-13). Dorcas was raised from the dead because Peter prayed (Acts 9:40-42).

Once we catch a glimpse of the amazing privilege and power of prayer, it is natural to wonder, "Why should God listen to me? I am no Moses, Joshua, or Peter." It is a good question. Not just anybody can pray and change the world. It is important to pause and ask, "Am I really praying in Jesus' name or am I really praying in my name." We must get this. The reason why things change

---

25 (L. T. C. Rolt, *Isambard Kingdom Brunel* [Harmondsworth, UK: Penguin, 1970], pp. 205-6).

when you and I pray is because we pray in Jesus' name. Through Jesus we have the ear of God, access to God, relationship to God, and the authority of God.

Few of us would expect that we could walk into our supervisor's office to ask for a raise or a change in our hours and be sure we would get what we ask for. Even fewer of us would expect that we could walk into the mayor's office and expect that our request would be granted. Or how about the president of the United States? Perhaps you might think, "Well that's ridiculous. Only those closest to the president could expect that." Exactly! Only those close to God expect to have their request taken seriously.

Our chances of getting a request granted from someone in authority are increased if we know someone who knows the boss, or the mayor, or the president. In my ministry against sexual misconduct I have had to speak to people whom I did not know and who had a great deal of authority. I looked for friends who trusted me and who could introduce me to those leaders. I have learned that whoever introduces me to someone in large measure determines how I am heard and viewed. That was true in meeting Cardinal O'Conner in his home at St. Patrick's Cathedral, true in meeting President Reagan in the White House, and true in talking with Mother Teresa.

About five years after the Billy Graham Crusade, I was increasingly concerned about the impact of pornography on my congregation and our country. I called the executive committee back together and asked them if they cared about what pornography was doing to their men. They said yes, so we met to study the issue that led to progress in shutting down sex businesses and pornography stores in Cincinnati.

During that time we were studying the impact of pornography, I had a powerful experience while memorizing the first chapter of Ephesians as a way of preparing for sermons I planned to preach through that year. When I got to verses 9 and 10, a passage we discussed earlier in this book, I read, "he made known to us the mystery of his will according to his good pleasure, which he purposed in Christ, to be put into effect when the times will have reached their fulfillment—to bring all things in heaven and earth together under one head, even Christ."

I got up from the table and began to pray. I remember my prayer like it was yesterday (although it was actually 1984). I said, "Father, if you intend to bring all things under Christ, surely you would like to get started now." Then I prayed, "You could even unite Presbyterians." I laughed. Then I prayed, "You could even unite the Southern Baptists." (They were meeting in Dallas that very day.) I laughed again and moved on to verse 11: "In him we were also chosen, having been predestined according to the plan of him who works out everything in conformity with the purpose of his will..." I saw clearly and with great conviction that God has a plan and he is God. He has the power to pull it off. I said to God, "You could even use the scourge of pornography to drive your people to their knees and to each other." In that moment I asked him to do it. And then I signed up for duty.

After that I called three leaders from the Billy Graham executive committee in Cincinnati. I asked them, "Do you believe we are called to impact only Cincinnati or the nation?" Their answer, of course, was "the nation." That led me to call Cardinal Joseph Bernadin. He had been archbishop in Cincinnati during the time of the Billy Graham Crusade. We had sat next to each other at an interdenominational dinner and continued meeting periodically after that, developing a deep bond as friends and prayer partners.

As the momentum to confront pornography on a national level grew, I knew I needed help. I was just a local pastor. So I called Cardinal Bernadin again. We were able to meet in Chicago while I was traveling, and again when he was visiting Cincinnati, and he was receptive and eager to help. We met for dinner, and of course the subject of pornography came up. He asked, "How can I help you?"

I said, "You could do three things." I didn't know exactly what they were when I began, but I launched out anyway and continued, "First, you could help me bring Christian leaders together to confront the issue of pornography, because they all know who you are and they don't know who I am. Second, you could help in educating the Catholic Church concerning pornography because it is affecting every denomination and will affect your denomination more and more. Third, you could help us prepare for an audience with Pope John Paul II because this is a worldwide problem and we need worldwide solutions."

He hesitated about fifteen seconds. Then he said, "I can do that." I almost fainted. I thought I was asking for the moon with each of the requests. He did not flinch from any of them. He could introduce me to Pope John Paul II, and he could introduce me to Mother Teresa. So the commitment was there, and it was a matter of logistics and timing.

Every six months I would call Joseph and ask him if this was the time to bring the leaders together. This went on for a couple of years. He said to me, "Every time you call me I am so embarrassed—but you are not here in Chicago screaming at me." I said, "Joseph, I will never be in Chicago screaming at you. When the time is right, we will know it."

On the way to speak in St. Louis, I stopped at a phone booth alongside the freeway and called him. "Is this the right time? The Attorney General's Commission on Pornography is going to give their report in July." This was mid-May 1986. He said, "There is a national meeting of bishops in a week. I will explore it with them. Call me back, and I will let you know."

When I called him back, he said, "I think this is the time. All the cardinals of the U.S. will meet at St. Patrick's Cathedral in late July. That would be the time to invite other leaders from across the country." He and Cardinal John J. O'Connor of New York would be pleased to cohost the meeting.

I could never have gotten through to the other cardinals. But because they trusted Cardinal Bernadin they were willing to meet. So we set up the meeting. I invited James Dobson to be one of the keynote speakers. Dr. Dobson was widely known because of his writing and radio program at Focus on the Family. (He now serves with Family Talk.)

If this group, which we eventually decided to call the *Religious Alliance Against Pornography*, was to have a significant impact, then it needed to be broad—covering the entire religious spectrum of our country. I did not know any Jewish leaders, but Billy Graham did. I went to him and asked him if he would introduce me to the leading rabbi in America. Although Dr. Graham was leading the Paris Crusade that week, he responded to my call and said, "Give me four days and I will prepare the way. The leader is Rabbi Tanenbaum. I will make contact and prepare him for your call." So four days later I called Rabbi Mark Tanenbaum, the head of the American Jewish Committee. I was delighted and amazed when he said, "Billy Graham has spoken to me and I have been waiting for your call. Could I invite some other leading rabbis to join us?"

After that I went to the top executives of many denominations: the Orthodox Church, the Episcopal Church, the Presbyterian Church, the United Methodist Church, the Southern Baptist Convention, the Church of the Nazarene, the Free Methodist Church, and many others. I went to the Mormons as well. They all agreed to come to our meeting in New York. I would not have had the gumption to call any of those people had I not memorized Ephesians 1:9-11 and believed it. I have been in over my head most of my life, and God takes me where I would not dare to go on my own.

In leading that meeting of the *Religious Alliance Against Pornography* in New York, I was the least known of any person present. Eventually, because of my belief in the power of God and the call to confront pornography, the *Religious Alliance Against Pornography* met with both President Reagan and Pope John Paul II in the Vatican. What was I doing in such exalted company? I was there because I was introduced by persons whom those leaders trusted: Cardinal Bernadin to Pope John Paul II and Mother Teresa; and Robert Showers, head of the obscenity section of the Justice Department Division, to Attorney General Meese, to President Reagan.

Now we are ready to see the way that this relates to praying in Jesus' name. Jesus has a personal relationship with his Father, and our chances of getting a hearing are vastly increased if Jesus authorizes our request. This is what Jesus is telling his disciples: "I tell you the truth, my Father will give you whatever you ask in my name. Until now you have not asked for anything in my name. Ask and you will receive, and your joy will be complete" (John 16:23, 24).

In the ancient world, not surprisingly, no one could just walk into the presence of the emperor. Access was only granted—even for the most privileged—to those who were led into the royal presence by an official called the Prosagos. Without the Prosagos, no soldiers would stand aside and the doors would not open; you were dead if you dared try to walk into the royal audience chamber alone. On the other hand, with the Prosagos in front of you, the guards stepped aside and the doors swung wide.

The apostle Paul describes Jesus as a Prosagos in his letter to the Christians at Ephesus. He assures them, "In him and through faith in him we may approach God with freedom and confidence" (Ephesians 3:12). Jesus takes us into the presence of God, and when Jesus leads us into God's presence, we approach God with confidence, because we are coming through official channels. Having assured the Ephesians that we have a Prosagos to the Father, Paul prays one of the most wonderful prayers in all of the Bible in Ephesians 3:14-21. I memorized this prayer many years ago, review it often, and have preached from it more than any passage in Scripture.

How sure were you as a child that what you asked of your parents would be granted? Probably not all the time, but if you had loving parents, you knew you had a good chance. Now, let's stretch the image a bit further. What assurance could you have had that what you asked from your next-door neighbor's parents might be granted? Not much. In fact, what right would you have had to ask anything of your neighbor's parents anyway? I can remember once trying to get something from my friend's parents by saying, "Billy (my neighbor) wants to know if we can have a candy bar." I was, literally, asking in Billy's name. It didn't work. Surprise, surprise!

Here is what we need to keep clearly in mind when it comes to prayer—God is our Creator who loves us. But he only becomes our Father when we receive his Son Jesus, are adopted as his children, and are regenerated by the Holy Spirit. We affirm this wonderful truth at the beginning of our Prayer Covenant when we say, "Dear Father, thank you for your grace that has made me one of your dearly loved children." We affirm this wonderful truth when we pray in the name of Jesus. "In Jesus' name" means that we are coming to God with our new identity. "Yet to all who received him, to those who believed in his name, he gave the right to become children of God— children born not of natural descent, nor of human decision or a husband's will, but born of God" (John 1:12-13). Jesus is the one who brings us to the Father.

AUTHORITY

When we pray in Jesus' name, in our new identity, we are praying with authority. Jesus' ministry begins with a declaration of his authority, as we saw earlier, when he announces, "The kingdom of God is near. Repent and believe the good news!" (Mark 1:15). He is the king, and what is it that a king needs in order to rule? He needs authority. He calls the disciples and they come (Mark 1:16-20); that's authority over people. He casts out demons (Mark 1:25); that's authority over evil. He heals people (Mark 1:34); that's authority over sickness. He calms a storm and walks on water (Mark 4:39-41, 6:45-52); that's authority over nature. He calls Lazarus from the tomb (John 11:43-44); that's authority over death.

It was Jesus' authority that most impressed people. If Jesus were to walk in your room right now, apart from his shining radiance, you would be struck with his authority. Those who heard him teach said, "What is this? A new teaching—and with authority!" (Mark 1:27).

The very last thing that Matthew tells us about Jesus relates to his authority: "All authority in heaven and on earth has been given to me" (Matthew 28:18). That's complete and total authority over everything that exists. When we get to heaven, we will see Jesus receiving worship with the Father on the throne: "To him who sits on the throne and to the Lamb be praise and honor and glory and power, for ever and ever!" (Revelation 5:13). That's eternal authority.

Jesus is the authority. And here is the point. Jesus gives his disciples authority to pray in his name. And that authority is for us, too. "And I will do whatever you ask in my name, so that the Son may bring glory to the Father. You may ask me for anything in my name, and I will do it" (John 14:13-14). "Until now you have not asked for anything in my name. Ask and you will receive, and your joy will be complete" (John 16:24).

It is precisely because of this authority of Jesus that the disciples continued the ministry of Jesus. Peter preached salvation in the name of Jesus: "Repent and be baptized, every one of you, in the name of Jesus Christ for the forgiveness of your sins. And you will receive the gift of the Holy Spirit" (Acts 2:38). And Peter healed in the name of Jesus: "Silver and gold I do not have, but what I do have I give you. In the name of Jesus Christ of Nazareth, walk" (Acts 3:6), and the lame man leaped up. And this healing ministry in the name of Jesus, by the authority of Jesus, continued through the ministry of the church in Acts, down through the centuries, and continues to this day. Christians live in the name of Jesus Christ. Christian ministry is in the authority of Jesus and is empowered as we pray in the authority of Jesus Christ.

When we see the authority of Jesus we understand the authority he has given us in prayer. It is belief in the authority of Jesus that has given me courage to challenge the depth of sexual sin in our society and to speak to people in places of leadership, far beyond my expectations.

Some of those meetings with authority figures have been wonderful. Some have been difficult confrontations.

It came to our attention that General Motors owned a cable company, Hughes Electronics, which was delivering pornography in homes across the country. The *Religious Alliance Against Pornography* and pureHOPE felt we should confront them. We were confident that we would be able to speak to them because we were such a broad coalition of leaders from across the entire religious spectrum. We could not be pigeonholed as narrow and reactionary. RAAP includes the entire spectrum of Christian, Jewish, and Muslim leaders.

First, we wrote a gracious letter to the president and CEO of General Motors. No response. So we wrote another letter, equally gracious but firm. Denis Beausejour had been Vice President for Global Marketing at Procter & Gamble, and he counseled us on ways to wisely approach them. We gathered signed petitions from around the country objecting strongly to General Motors's participation in the pornography industry. With each letter we sent ten thousand signed petitions. We did this for three successive months and told them we would do so every month until they were out of the pornography business. The third month we told them the time had come for us to hold a press conference and tell the nation that GM was in the pornography business. That third letter got a response. They flew a team of executives to meet with us in Cincinnati. I was proud of our team. Everyone was businesslike but firm. Shortly after that meeting, we received a letter telling us that they were selling the company and getting out of the pornography business.

Our courage to take on a multinational corporation grew from our confidence that God has given authority to confront evil wherever it appears. And pornography is an evil that is attacking our young people, marriages, and families. The time has come when all Christians and people of faith must confront the growing sex industry that fuels the sex trafficking of our young people. This is the new slavery that must not be tolerated. Do you believe that when you pray, you pray in the authority of Jesus Christ? If you don't, your prayers will be powerless. If you do, you will be praying in power, and you will see answers to prayer that will produce the fruit of the Spirit.

Remember, the question underlying all prayer is, "Why should God listen to me?" What right do we have to think God would listen to my small prayers? This may sound humble, but this is a false humility, because we are not thinking of ourselves correctly. In Christ, we are children of God. God is our Father and Jesus is our Lord. Therefore we have the right to pray, and even the responsibility to pray, with the confidence that we will be heard.

FAITH

Scripture says that "without faith it is impossible to please God" (Hebrews 11:6). Without faith it is impossible to pray in Jesus' name, too. Faith is the activating ingredient for prayer. Jesus told the disciples, "If you believe, you will receive whatever you ask for in prayer" (Matthew 21:22). We are talking here not about assent to the teachings of the Christian faith; we are talking about trusting in what we believe and in whom we believe. It is not enough to know that God hears prayer. You must pray with the conviction that your prayer will be received. There is a pervasive confidence we are to have; this is not arrogance. We pray, not because we believe we are worthy to be heard by God, but because we believe what Jesus tells us and that he is worthy. Perhaps a helpful word here is trust. Believing with trust leads to prayers that are clearly audacious and even risky, yet they are prayers that get answered. And they are kingdom of God prayers. They are not just for self. They are for the kingdom of God and are to be consistent with the character and ministry of Jesus.

The work of the *Religious Alliance Against Pornography* was one of the primary influences that eventually led to the strongest legislation in our country against obscenity, enacted during the Reagan Administration. The courage to take on pornography was made possible because we were introduced to people who had the authority to make a difference, but it also grew from a sense of faith that God would act.

One morning I was reading in the Gospel of Matthew and praying out on our enclosed porch. I was captivated by Jesus' parable of the one lost sheep and these words in Matthew 18:14: "In the same way your Father in heaven is not willing that any of these little ones should be lost." That verse grabbed my heart, because I had just learned the FBI statistic that one out of every seven little boys and one of every three little girls would be molested by the age of eighteen.

I used to go up the hill across from our house regularly to pray. This time those statistics were ringing in my mind, and I became angry with myself, with the church, and finally angry with God. I was overwhelmed and began to cry. The pain of children being molested and God's people doing nothing to protect them was unbearable. I said to God, "You tell me that you love the little children, why don't you do something? You tell me you love the little children, why—don't—you—do something?"

I must have said that prayer five or six times as I walked up the hill, and each time louder and more firmly than before. By the time I reached the top of the hill I was weeping convulsively. Finally, I said to the Lord, "Don't tell me you love these children. SHOW ME!" By this time I was shouting. "I don't want words any more. I want action. I want you to show me that you love them." I knew I was verging on the edge of blasphemy. But I wanted to believe that God would act.

Then I became silent before God. By this time I was cried out. I was prayed out and worn out. Then these words came to me. I didn't hear any voice. "Jerry, I love these little children. But I have chosen to love them through my people. Why don't you do something?" The impression was so strong that I repeated those words to myself as often as I had asked the question. At first the burden on my heart was so great I could hardly stand it. I had a sense of responsibility and calling that was crushing me. Then I said to the Lord, "I cannot bear this burden alone. Either you have to give this burden for the protection of children and families to others as well, or you have to lift it from me. Lord, only you can do this." The weight of the call connected with my natural sense of inadequacy and my limited abilities.

Then I relaxed because I believed. I believed that God was going to do it. He loves the children, and he will do it through his people, and I was going to have a small part in that. That sense of faith in God's promise to act set me free. After that I called Charles Keating, who had been on the first Attorney General's Commission

Against Pornography. He cared deeply and opened doors for people to join in the battle, especially Carl Lindner Jr. Carl became my friend and partner in the battle, faithfully providing funding and support for the effort. Through him I made a contact that resulted in financial support for both pureHOPE and the *Religious Alliance Against Pornography* so that the ministries could move forward.

Faith leads us to act and to reach beyond what we can naturally do. I know that my request for a million people to pray the Prayer Covenant is a big request. But it is only an initial request. Do you think those million could remain silent about the Lord and about the Prayer Covenant? Do you think it will end with them? Do you believe that their believing God will not move them out to invite others, many others to join them, rejoicing in the grace and forgiveness of God, love for God and others, and a passion to follow Jesus as Lord? Will they not focus on living for the glory of God by "following Jesus together" and by inviting others to join them in that adventure with genuine dependence upon the Holy Spirit?

But I believe that this is a God-pleasing way to pray. I have written that the Prayer Covenant is a dangerous prayer. Well, that faith which empowers our prayers is a dangerous faith. It is a trust that lets us move from the side of the pool to the middle, and from the shallows into the deep end.

I have a friend, Doug, who describes the prayer of faith as "putting your hands in the air." He hates roller coasters. When his sons were young he lived in Florida, not far from Disney World. Once when Doug's in-laws came to visit, they all decided to spend the day at the park. Of course his sons, ages four, nine, and eleven, and Doug's father-in-law, George, picked the roller coaster ride Space Mountain as their first choice. Doug was not enthusiastic, but he agreed to go on the ride because he didn't want to be left out. The line was long, and it took almost an hour to wind their way up to the top. The closer they came to the launch area, the worse he felt. But since even his four-year-old couldn't wait, he did his best to join in the fun.

When they were strapped in the cars, his youngest son, Justin, was seated with George in the front compartment, while Doug was seated in the back compartment by himself. As the brake was released, the car went whipping down the coaster track with drops and rises, jolting from side to side. Doug sat in the back with his teeth gritted, hands gripping the sides of the car, merely enduring the descent. In the front compartment it was entirely different. George and Justin were howling with laughter, their hands lifted high in the air. They were having the time of their lives. There was no reason for Doug's anxiety. The ride was completely safe, and millions of people had gone down the track. He knew that if he could have just relaxed he could have enjoyed it, too.

It was this memory that came back to him in a time of prayer when he was seeking God's guidance. He stood at a fork in his career and was not sure what to do. Whichever fork he took there would be challenges, dangers, and risks. As he was praying, it was as if the Lord said to him, "Son, you are going down, and there are going to be drops, rises, and jolts that are going to knock you about. However, you are completely safe as I have you in my hand. But you have to trust me. You are going down. Don't grit your teeth or grip the sides. Put your hands in the air."

No matter what you are facing, when you pray, put your hands in the air. This is the kind of faith with which God wants us to pray. We are to believe him; to trust him for all that will happen. He wants us to stop gritting our teeth and gripping the sides for dear life. More than that, we are to have such faith that we can put our hands in the air and laugh on the way down.

How much are you willing to believe and pray for? Don't be afraid. Pray small prayers, and even more, pray big prayers. Someone once commented: if we only pray for what we can achieve by our efforts, our prayers are probably insulting to God.

INTENTION

To pray in Jesus' name affirms that we are living for the purposes of Jesus Christ, not merely our own selfish desires. We are saying that we want the intention of our lives to be pleasing to God. Think back through some of the requests in the Prayer Covenant. They are all about our intentions. To pray in Jesus' name means that we are affirming that we want Jesus to "be Lord of my life today in new ways, and change me any way you want"! To pray in Jesus' name means we are saying, "Use me today for your glory." To pray in Jesus' name is to desire to be used as an instrument of God's grace, truth, forgiveness, righteousness, and justice.

To dig deeper into praying in Jesus' name, we must keep in mind the original context of Jesus' teaching about prayer in John 13–17, what Bible commentators call the Upper Room Discourse. Jesus was about to depart to heaven by means of the cross. The disciples were about to be sent on their mission. How could they carry on the work of the kingdom of God without Jesus? The assuring answer was by means of the Holy Spirit and prayer. For the work Jesus assigned them they could ask for what they needed and be assured that they would receive it. But they had to ask in Jesus' name.

As a pastor and leader of various ministries, I have been given expense accounts for the cost of doing ministry. The money in the account is not mine. But I am authorized to use it for whatever I need as long as it furthers the ministry. When I travel to a conference or buy anything that I use for ministry, even down to paper and ink, I don't have to take it out of my family's income. I can spend money in the name of our church or ministry. Having an expense account gives me a great deal of freedom. But the expense account has conditions. I must not use it for my personal benefit or for my family. For instance, I can't put my family in the car and take a vacation on ministry funds.

This promise of prayer in Jesus' name is similar. Our Lord promises the resources we need as we serve him. All we need to do is ask. We can have great confidence, since there are supernatural resources available to us. The condition for getting the help from heaven is that we must ask for things in Jesus' name, that is, according to his character, purpose, and plan.

Of course our prayer requests are not just about doing ministry. We can ask for our daily bread—whatever we need to live. Yet when we ask for personal needs, we must keep in mind that the focus of our lives is not personal gratification but obedience to the will of our Lord. We see this clearly in the Lord's Prayer. Before we ask for our daily bread, we pray that God's name would be revered, that his kingdom would come, and his will would be done (Matthew 6:9-10). This way of praying transforms us. It reshapes our thinking. It turns us away from self-centeredness. We don't serve ourselves; we serve the Lord. Even Jesus kept his personal desires in perspective in prayer. In the Garden of Gethsemane, Jesus said, "Not my will, but yours be done" (Luke 22:42).

SINCERITY

All our prayers end with "Amen." Why do we do this? First, let's be clear that "Amen" is not a magical formula. The word *Amen* derives from Hebrew and means to confirm, support, establish, or verify. When we say "Amen," we are declaring that we are serious—we really mean it.

The use of the word *Amen* at the end of any prayer is a challenge to us. How easily prayer becomes routine and even insincere. From time to time I catch myself saying the Lord's Prayer with a wandering mind. Like most of us, I know it so well that even while I am praying it my mind drifts to something else. At that point, my praying becomes insincere—mixed. I am pretty sure that Jesus would describe this as hypocritical praying. What Jesus wants from me is a pure heart and a pure prayer that is focused on God from the depths of my being. Distracted prayers are not God-honoring prayers. When I say "Amen," I am declaring that my prayer is sincere. When I say "Amen," I am saying this prayer is certified as honest and true. When we say "in Jesus' name. Amen," in the Prayer Covenant, we are saying that we pray this prayer not in a casual way or distracted manner but with passion, purpose and faith. We are not merely praying it out of religious duty. We are not praying thoughtlessly or routinely. We are saying it because we mean it.

One of my prayer partners lived in England for a couple of years. He observed that the phrase "in the name of Jesus" is used differently in Britain than in the US. In most American prayer meetings it is customary for several people to offer prayers, and then someone concludes the entire prayer time by saying, "in the name of Jesus, Amen."

In the British prayer meeting, after *each* person prayed, the conclusion of their prayer would be "in the name of Jesus," a slight pause, and then everyone would chime in with a resounding *"Amen!"* In a typical prayer meeting, "in the name of Jesus" was used frequently—that was powerful. But what really stuck with him was the repeated and resounding *"Amen!"* that punctuated the entire prayer meeting. The point was to remind you that everyone was with you as you were with them, affirming one another's prayer.

That experience shapes how he prays the Prayer Covenant for his partners—he has quite a few. He concludes with a resounding *"Amen!"* after each and every person he prays for. In this way each person gets an affirmation, a declaration, and a sealing of the prayer covenant.

Jonathan Edwards wrote about the state of the heart that I believe is embodied in the word *Amen* this way:

> That religion which God requires, and will accept, does not consist in weak, dull and lifeless wishes, raising us but a little above a state of indifference; God, in his word, greatly insists upon it, that we be in good earnest, fervent in spirit; and our hearts vigorously engaged in religion.[26]

That spirit of seeking God with passion is what we are affirming when we say, "in the name of Jesus. *Amen.*"

---

26 (*The Religious Affections* [Edinburgh, UK: Banner of Truth Trust, 1986], p. 27)

REFLECTION QUESTIONS

Chapter 11   Authority

1. How is praying in Jesus' name different than having "good thoughts" towards another person and wishing them well?

2. Why is it important to give careful consideration to what it means to pray in Jesus' name? Why can't we just pray in our own name?

3. It was when I *believed* what I read about Jesus' authority that I was prepared to risk exposing the devastation of pornography in people's lives and pointing them to the grace of Christ. How can this understanding of faith and believing empower your prayer life?

4. Praying in Jesus' name means praying within the purpose and mission of Jesus. How does this focus clarify that for which we should and should not pray?

5. What's the difference between praying a half-hearted prayer and declaring that you are praying in Jesus' name?

COVENANTING

NOW THAT YOU HAVE LEARNED about each line of the Prayer Covenant, your next step is to join in a Prayer Covenant with one or several others. In this chapter we will consider how to invite someone into the Prayer Covenant and how to follow up once you have begun.

Before we look at these practical steps, I want to remind you of the benefits of the Prayer Covenant and what makes it so special. Before I began to pray the Prayer Covenant I was already a dedicated Christian; I had led people to Christ; I had started two Young Life clubs in Seattle; I had asked to be filled with the Holy Spirit; I had dedicated my life to Christ again and again. I had been to seminary; I had pastored two churches for ten years; I was the chairman of the evangelism committee for my presbytery. What was life-changing then was that Don Rehberg asked me to commit my life to Jesus as Lord every day and to be accountable for it. It was the regularity and the accountability that was new. This was following Jesus together. This was living out Luke 9:23, in which Jesus says that we are to take up our cross and follow him "daily."

Within two weeks of entering into that first Prayer Covenant with Don, I invited a woman in my church in New Wilmington to enter into the Prayer Covenant with me. As her pastor, she had told me that her marriage was falling apart. I told her about the Prayer Covenant: "Let's pray and then see what the Lord will do." Two weeks later she came to me and said, "I can't pray that prayer. Jerry, I didn't tell you the whole truth. I am the one having the affair."

I responded, "Do you think that your not being able to pray the prayer was an answer to our prayers?" She thought about it and said, "Maybe it was."

Then I asked, "Do you think maybe that you are ready to pray the prayer, now that you have shared with me your struggle?" She said yes. So we entered into the Prayer Covenant a second time. Two weeks later she broke off the relationship with the other man. Two years later she and her husband came from New Wilmington to College Hill to tell me of God's blessing and of her healthy relationship with her husband. This experience, and many more, helped build my confidence in the Prayer Covenant.

If you are going to invite others into the Prayer Covenant, then you too need to have confidence in it. It is important that you pray the prayer for a week or two, and maybe more, so you have a sense of it affecting your life in general and specific ways. This will enable you to share with passion and confidence. We need a sense of change in our lives through praying it, a sense of growing, a sense of joy in the Lord, a sense of praise welling up from within us.

The more of God's grace that fills your life, the greater motivation you will have for sharing the good news about God's grace through this prayer with others. The more you fill your life with God's compassion for people and their struggles and needs, the more you will be prepared to share with others. The more you allow the Spirit to convict you of your sins, the more you will identify with others in their struggles and sins. Remember the old saying is true: "It is one beggar telling another beggar where there is food to be had." In praying for someone else, it is not the strong helping the weak. It is not one person who has found the Holy Grail and has finally arrived to help poor sinners find it too. Humility and a servant spirit open the door to covenant prayer with integrity.

The more faithfully and deeply you worship the Lord, the greater your preparation. With growing confidence you will be ready for

God to use you to touch others. It will be helpful to read the Gospels so that you can connect with Jesus through his teachings, and reading them will help you cultivate the sense of his presence. Read especially Matthew 5–7, the Sermon on the Mount, and John 13–17, the Upper Room Discourse—more than once! If you could memorize key verses from them, that would be even better. Spend time in the Psalms, too. Verses 1 and 3 of Psalm 34 are special verses to me. "O magnify the Lord with me, and let us exalt his name together" (Psalm 34:3 RSV) has been our family verse for the past twenty-five years.

Ask God to fill you with his Holy Spirit and believe his promise to do so. This too prepares us for sharing the Prayer Covenant. Get to know these verses on the Holy Spirit: John 7:37-39; 16:7; Acts 1:8; and Ephesians 5:17-18. These verses will give you a growing sense of dependence on the Spirit and his power in and through you. Become familiar with 1 Corinthians 6:19: "Do you not know that your bodies are temples of the Holy Spirit, who is in you, whom you have received from God? You are not your own." It is that sense of the Spirit that gives us boldness, confidence, and freedom to share. Believe that God intends to and will use you.

One of the benefits of praying the Prayer Covenant daily is that the individual lines of the prayer begin to lodge in your heart. I find them coming to mind throughout the day. For instance, as I meet with someone, I will find myself quietly asking the Lord, "Empower me to love others the way that you love me." As I am driving in my car or taking a walk I find myself saying, "I will praise you, O Lord, with all my heart." Or from out of nowhere I will become aware of how far short of God's grace I have fallen and will say, "Wash me clean from every sin." There is power in each of these prayers.

INVITING

Once you have been praying the prayer for a week or two, you are ready to invite someone to join you. However, before you begin inviting, you need to have a story. It is important that you can say to someone, "This is how the Prayer Covenant is affecting me."

When you prepare to speak to someone about the Prayer Covenant, consider which line of the prayer is having the greatest impact on your life. In what ways has it changed you? How has it increased your faith? This is the time to share your story.

Perhaps it is the line on worship that has most deeply affected you; be prepared to tell how it changed your level of worship and your desire for worship. Perhaps it is the request to be more loving to others. How is it changing your capacity for compassion? Your sensitivity to others' needs?

You have been praying that Jesus be Lord of your life in new ways. In what ways are you more aware of Jesus and his life in you? Of his presence, his will, his blessing, his power? In what ways are you thinking about Jesus more and more during the day?

Think about how you have asked God to use you for his glory and to make you his instrument. Look for ways that God is indeed using you for his glory. This will increase your confidence. You have asked for more understanding of his work in you and through you for grace, truth, forgiveness, righteousness, and justice. Look for his work through you; expect it.

Now you are ready to extend the invitation. Whom do we start with? Choose one, two, or three of the most dedicated people you know. Tell them you want to follow Jesus together. You are inviting them to pray for themselves, and you are asking them to pray for you. You will do the same. That is what makes it easy to grow.

You might want to start by inviting a family member to pray with and for you. How about someone at your church? Maybe someone in a Sunday School class or on a church board? Perhaps even one of the pastors? Possibly one or two of your closest friends? Begin with the people you know are most eager to grow spiritually. Maybe you could begin with new Christians. Perhaps you could look for people who have just responded to a powerful sermon where there is a stirring of the Spirit. Maybe a colleague at work whom you know loves the Lord.

Or it might be wise to start with Christians who are more mature than you but are not as excited about the Lord as you are. They will help you feel most comfortable to share the Prayer Covenant. Let them know you respect them because of the depth of their knowledge and commitment. Tell them you are not coming to them because you can help them but because they can help you. You need their maturity. I have found that those most mature in the Lord are those most eager to take another step forward in their commitment to Christ. You may discern that they need your fire, but you don't need to say so.

I look for two qualities in persons with whom I want to enter in the Prayer Covenant, faithfulness and fire. There are people who are faithful but have not fire. And there are people who have fire but are shallow. I seek out those who bring those two wonderful qualities together.

Pray regularly ahead of time for those with whom you want to share the Prayer Covenant. Sometimes I have prayed for people a week, a month or even for over a year before I invited them to join me in a prayer covenant. I have a friend, Lou Shirey, who is the Director of Pastoral Development and Prayer in the International Pentecostal Holiness Denomination. He encourages pastors of churches that are going to use the Prayer Covenant to suggest to their members that they pray the Prayer for at least 10 days before entering into prayer covenants with each other.

Don't be in a hurry. God is building his kingdom. There are no emergencies in the kingdom of God. Listening skills are crucial. Spend much of your time listening when you invite someone into the Prayer Covenant. It helps to ask questions in order to get better acquainted with them.

You may want to invite someone out to have a cup of coffee. As you are sitting down together, spend much of the initial time listening so that they are the center of attention and you get to know them much better. Then ask them if you could share something that is blessing your life. If they say, "Yes," you are ready to tell your story about how the Prayer Covenant became a part of your life and how it is impacting you. Then you are ready to invite them to join you. Take out your Prayer Covenant Card and show it to them. Have a Prayer Covenant Card to give them as well. Point out both the one-word summary of each line, and then point out the full text of each request. Again, don't be in a hurry. Let them look over the Prayer Covenant Card and then encourage them to make comments or ask questions. I almost always ask them to pray about whether they want to enter the Prayer Covenant with me rather than invite them directly at that time. God will give you direction and discernment about how to proceed.

You might even want to have a copy of this book to pass on so they can read about the Prayer Covenant. Or perhaps that might be overkill! Be sensitive. I am reminded of a young seminarian who was to preach his first sermon at a small country church. Since this was his first sermon, he prepared even more carefully—working at least thirty hours in study and carefully outlining his remarks. He arrived half an hour early. No one was there when he arrived, but he found what appeared to be a pastor's study, so he went into pray and further prepare. Just before 11:00 a.m., he came out from the study and discovered only one person sitting in a pew.

He approached the lone attender and said, "I've noticed that it is time to begin. I have prepared. Should I go ahead or should we cancel the service?" The man said, "Well, son, I'm from the country. If'n I was to take a load of hay out to the cows and only one cow showed up, I don't think I would turn that cow away." That seemed right, so the seminary student led worship and preached. After preaching for half an hour, he discovered that he was only halfway through his sermon. So he paused and asked his listener, "I just noticed my watch and realized I have been preaching for thirty minutes and I am only halfway through my sermon. Should I keep going or finish up?" The man sitting in the pew said, "Well, son, I'm from the country. If'n I was to take a load of hay out to feed the cows and only one cow showed up, I don't think I would give him the whole load."

So, again, be sensitive. Tell your friends that, if they choose, you will pray each day through the Prayer Covenant for yourself and then pray for them. If you are only in a few Prayer Covenants, you will find it very powerful to pray through every line of the prayer for each person. As you pray through the lines of the prayer repeatedly, you will find they are working their way deeper into your heart even as they bring power to those for whom you pray. Since

I am in many Prayer Covenants, I no longer pray the entire prayer over each person. Instead I pray one of the following lines about or from the prayer: "Seal the Prayer in _____'s life today." Or, "Jesus, be Lord of _____ today in new ways." Or, "Jesus, please fill _____ with your Holy Spirit."

Tell them you are committing to pray for them daily and that you are inviting them to do the same for you. Further, tell them that you want to be accountable. That means either during the period of the Prayer Covenant or shortly after it is over, you will be checking in, both to honor the commitment of accountability and more importantly just to hear about what God is doing in their life. In your time together, keep in mind above all: humility! Humility! And humility! God is the one who changes lives. We don't. You are not the authority. You are a fellow struggler and a fellow disciple.

Once you have entered into a Prayer Covenant with one or more people, you have only just begun. Expand your vision. Keep in mind that the Prayer itself encourages your prayer partners to invite others to pray the Prayer Covenant as well. You not only want to be a partner or, in some cases, a spiritual parent, but you also want to be a grandparent through the Prayer Covenant. It's wonderful to parent; it's even better to be a grandparent; it is even better than that to be a great-grandparent!

Our goal is for the Prayer Covenant to be a catalyst for being discipled and for discipling others as a way of life. I don't want people to come to the point where they say, "Well I've prayed the Prayer Covenant, now, what's next?" Let's not turn the Prayer Covenant into the next new fad, program or spiritual technique. I have prayed the essence of this Prayer for forty five years.

The Prayer Covenant is a tool to encourage fellow Christians to follow Jesus together, as a way of life, all our lives. When I say, "all our lives," please don't be overwhelmed. An essential dynamic of the Prayer Covenant is that it is both limited and lasting. Once you have finished forty days of prayer you can just move on when you are ready. There are always other brothers and sisters in Christ with whom you can pray.

As you discover and share God's work through the Prayer Covenant, there is no need to rush. I have a friend who likes to say, "There are no emergencies in the Kingdom of God." God is interested in a lasting movement, not a wildfire that leaves people excited for the moment but burned out and used up. When I am tempted to get in a hurry to get lots of people, right away, to join in the Prayer Covenant, I remind myself of the B.S. / B.S. principles — Build Slowly, Build Solidly. What matters is the long-term impact of the Prayer Covenant to exalt Christ. What matters is the glory of God through a deepening and lasting movement to exalt Christ as Lord. God is already at work. As we pray the Prayer Covenant with others we join a movement of God already under way.

FOLLOW UP

Follow-up is important. We all need the boost that comes from being accountable to another. If you never follow up, what's the point of accountability? When we do follow up, we must keep in mind that this is not some sort of inspection—never as a supervisor to an employee. It is one colleague to another, fellow passenger to fellow passenger.

So how do you follow up? Perhaps it is with a phone call at an appropriate time, or perhaps meeting for another cup of coffee. Sometimes I don't follow up for a long period of time. Whenever I do make contact, I let them know that I kept praying for them past the forty days. My questions are open-ended rather than closed (ones that can be answered with simply yes or no). I ask something like, "I want to know, what is God doing in your life?" Or I may say, "How would you describe the impact of the Prayer Covenant in your life," or, "In what ways have you shared the Prayer Covenant with others?" Perhaps it's, "You know I have been praying a version of this prayer for a long time. How have you been praying it?" I don't do the same thing every time. I need variety. However it happens, I always look forward to these follow-up calls. I can hardly wait to get back with the Prayer Covenant partners to find out what God has been doing.

I am in many Prayer Covenants all the time. And I am always looking for who's next. I average about one new Prayer Covenant a day or every other day. One of the great things I love about this is that I am invited into the hearts of God's people and I have many godly people praying for me that Jesus will be Lord of my life in new ways. I believe this is the great secret of the spiritual blessings and fruit God has given in my life and ministry. There are lots of people praying for me all the time, even as I get to pray for lots of people to follow Jesus and to grow in serving the Lord.

How much time do I spend going to new people and how much time do I spend following up on others? I don't keep track. But I work on this all the time, because I am asking God for an awakening to Jesus Christ as Lord throughout the United States and the world. I know that a five-minute call two weeks after the conversation is worth a half-hour call two months later. I know that a ten-minute call three weeks later is worth an hour three months later. There are some Prayer Covenant partners I speak with almost every week. For many, the Prayer Covenant doesn't end after forty days, it just continues.

Sometimes I may stop praying for others at the end of the Prayer Covenant only to discover that my partners have continued to pray for me. Years ago I entered into a Prayer Covenant with Dr. Myers Hicks at a conference in Montreat, North Carolina. He was an elder in a church not too far from there. Ten years later I was back at a conference in Montreat, and he was there too. He sought me out and told me what God had been doing in his life. Then he said, "I have prayed for you every day for these ten years." I said, "Oh Myers, that is so humbling. You only got thirty days. I got all those freebies."

A few years ago I received a phone call from Kent Smith, a former member of College Hill who had moved to Dallas. He asked me what God was doing in my life. Then he said, "I have prayed for you every day for twenty-seven years." I was overwhelmed. I responded to him the same way I did to Myers Hicks: "Kent, I only prayed for you for thirty days." He said, "Jerry, you brought me to Christ. It is my privilege to pray for you." That is so humbling and so encouraging.

PRAYING

Perhaps the best thing about the Prayer Covenant is that it reminds us and guides us to pray. Whether we are young Christians or mature Christians, keeping our prayer life fresh, vital, and constant is a challenge. And yet, as Christians, praying is our real work.

Richard Foster writes, "All who have walked with God have viewed prayer as the main business of their lives."[27] I needed to know that—it changed my priorities. I thought I was walking with God but prayer was not the main business of my life.

While we know that prayer is essential, we wander from it. We have to return to it again and again. I have a friend who describes the "just a minute" syndrome: "When I sit down to pray, my eye will catch a magazine article that I want to read. I read the article, telling myself I'll get back to my prayers in just a minute. But somehow I seldom do." Another reason that we find it difficult to pray is that we think we have too much to do. What we fail to understand is that only with prayer can we accomplish the most important things in life. Martin Luther once said, "I have so much to do today that I will have to spend an extra hour in prayer."

Thomas Kelly, in his book *Testament of Devotion*, puts the struggle between work and prayer in proper perspective: "We need not worry that this work will take up too much of our time, for it takes no time, but it occupies all our time. We order our mental life on two levels. One level we may be thinking, discussing, seeing and meeting various demands. At a profounder level, we may be worshipping, praying and listening."[28]

I recently received an email from Judy Haag, one of my Prayer Covenant partners. She apologized for having dropped the ball on her prayers for me. I wrote her back and said, "Well it's a 40 Day commitment. It's ok with me if it takes you 50 days or so to get it all in."

---

27 (*Celebration of Discipline* [San Francisco: Harper and Row, 1987], p. 32).
28 (quoted in *Celebration of Discipline*, p. 45).

The point I want to make here is that we must not be legalistic. While we are committed and accountable to one another, we also need to be gracious. Without grace we can become bound up in knots of guilt. It is possible to miss a few days and then feel so guilty that we stop praying altogether.

Praying the Prayer Covenant with others is a great joy and also real work. I have found that keeping time set aside for worship and prayer to be like digging a hole in water. It just keeps filling back up. The pace of our lives and the expectations of others will always compete for time with God. We can relax as we remember that God's love for us is not dependent upon how much or how little we pray.

In keeping our prayer covenant there is both discipline and desire. We do have to be disciplined; that means we must be conscious of competing demands and know when to say "Enough!" What keeps our discipline fresh and enriching rather than drudgery is that we really do want to spend time with God and we really do desire to pray for others.

MAKING A DIFFERENCE

The Prayer Covenant is a tool to aid you in connecting with God and serving him in this world. Our world is in great need. Whether we look at the world with an international or national perspective or on a personal level, there are pains and problems everywhere. If you knew one thing that you could do to make a difference, would you do it? Of course! And what is the one thing you could do that would make a difference? Almost every one of us, after just a little reflection, would say "prayer." But how many of us actually pray for the things that we lament? How many of us pray as if the state of the world were dependent upon our prayers?

Prayer is so simple and yet so difficult. Prayer is something that the youngest Christian can do right away, and yet it is something that the most mature believers must continue to work at. Prayer is a challenge for many reasons. When we pray, we engage in warfare with the major assumptions of our world today. Prayer makes no sense in a world that discounts the spiritual side of life. Prayer makes no sense in a world in which success is achieved only through our own diligent efforts. Prayer makes no sense in our self-centered world, in which we are encouraged to put ourselves ahead of all others. Prayer makes no sense in a world in which God has been exiled to the edges of life.

Prayer leads us into a different way of living. When we pray, we step into the heavenly realms. When we pray, we are drawing upon divine power to address challenges that cannot be achieved by our efforts alone. When we pray, we go beyond our own personal concerns to lift up the needs of others. When we pray, we acknowledge that God is the center of all of life and has power to work his will and achieve his purposes. When we pray we are partnering with God at the deepest level. "In prayer, real prayer, we begin to think God's thoughts after him: To desire the things he desires, to love the things he loves, to will the things he wills."[29]

Prayer makes things happen in us and in the world. It is almost shocking to say, but I know that it is true—prayer changes what God does in the world. More than that, prayer changes the world,

---

29 (Foster, *Celebration of Discipline*, p. 33).

and prayer changes those who pray. Prayer is the missing puzzle piece; prayer is the key that unlocks closed doors; prayer makes the Bible come alive for you; prayer makes sense of the Christian life.

Even as we pray, we have much to learn about prayer. Richard Foster writes that he put all the teachings of Jesus on prayer side-by-side so he could read them at one time:

> When I could read Jesus' teaching on prayer at one sitting, I was shocked. Either the excuses and rationalizations for unanswered prayer I had been taught were wrong, or Jesus' words were wrong. I determined to learn to pray so that my experience conformed to the words of Jesus rather than try to make His words conform to my impoverished experience.[30]

I have memorized most of these words of Jesus and most of the other promises of God on the power of prayer. I often review them when I pray and they are leading me to believe God for a Christ awakening.

One of the great teachers of the Christian church through the centuries was Augustine of Hippo. He writes of prayer:

> Holy prayer is the column of all virtues; a ladder to God; the support of widows, the foundation of faith; the crown of religion; the sweetness of the married life... Prayer is the protection of holy souls... an insupportable torment to the devil, a most acceptable homage to God... the greatest honor and glory, the preserver of spiritual health.[31]

After being a pastor for thirty years, God called me to confront

---

30 (*Celebration of Discipline*, p. 37)
31 (*Auct. Serm. ad. Fratres in eremo apud*, Serm. 22)

the sexualizing of our culture. When it was time to retire from pureHOPE, I was discouraged for two or three hours. But then came a new call—The Prayer Covenant. I am so grateful to God that you have read this book and are preparing to join in Prayer Covenants with others. I am filled with hope for what God is going to do in this world as millions of us covenant together to seek God. What a difference we will see! Following Jesus together in prayer is one of the greatest joys of the Christian life and brings untold blessings of eternity right into the midst of our needy world. To God be the glory!

REFLECTION QUESTIONS

Chapter 12   Covenanting

1. Before you consider asking someone to enter a Prayer Covenant with you, it would be good to reflect on it. How many of the lines can you recall without looking at the Prayer Covenant Card? Are there one or two lines that have been particularly meaningful?

2. In what ways have you noticed God working in your life since you began to pray the Prayer Covenant? (This becomes your time to share as you invite others to join the Prayer Covenant.)

3. As you seek to be led by the Spirit who are the people you want to invite to enter the Prayer Covenant? (Make a list of their names and begin to pray for them ahead of time. In some cases I have prayed months and even over a year before inviting them to join me in the prayer.)

4. How are you going to invite? Are you going to invite someone out for coffee, talk for a while after church, call someone on the phone or send an email? (Don't be in a hurry. God is building his kingdom and he has all the time in the world.)

5. Consider; how are you going to be in contact with your Prayer Covenant Partners during the forty days? (It would be good to order or download Prayer Cards that you can pass on. Also, be sure to exchange phone number and email address.)

MY JOURNEY IN PRAYER   Rick Schatz

Jerry's introduction of Rick Schatz

I have "followed Jesus together" with Rick Schatz since the early 70's when I had the privilege of leading him to Christ—he was then a student at the Harvard Business School. Our lives have been woven together since then, first at College Hill Presbyterian Church and then in the ministry of pureHOPE as he became my partner and Chief Executive Officer. Rick is a man of faith and faithfulness to whom I trust my life in the Lord. He is my brother and accountability partner in the deepest sense.

I am grateful that he is willing to share his prayer patterns with you in this concluding postscript. I am challenged and encouraged by him and I believe that you will be as well. As you will read, he spends an hour every day with the Lord, in the middle of the night! The Lord wakes him up and he gets up! Not only does he get up to spend time with the Lord, he has kept a prayer journal daily for over twenty years. I believe that a healthy devotional life requires both discipline (I do it because I have made a commitment) and desire (I do it because it nourishes my soul). From his example I hope you will see how that balance of discipline and desire can work together to enrich your own prayer life. I think I should let you know that I find his example helpful because I have started and stopped writing prayer journals over the years. Rick's example encourages me to do it again.

I was not raised in a Christian home, but like all good people, we went to church on Christmas and Easter whether we needed to or not. My experience with prayer was a 30-second grace before dinner, but I certainly had no personal relationship with the Lord or devotional life at all.

When I came to Christ at the beginning of my second year at the Harvard Business School, I figured there would be two things I should begin to do immediately. First was to read the Bible, the second was to pray. With the Bible reading, I started in Genesis and got about halfway through Leviticus and gave up, wondering, what in the world was this book all about? My commitment to begin to pray was met with similar disappointment and frustration.

Despite the fact that I heard many sermons on prayer and the need for all Christians to pray, my lack of success lasted for many years. The sermons I heard focused on Jesus' prayer life and the disciples praying regularly and fervently with great faith, but the impact was simply guilt and shame and more frustration. But all that began to change through some great teaching and the development of some tools that have produced lasting positive results.

The teaching came through Dick Eastman. He had a program called "The Hour That Changes the World." His focus was on praying for missionaries and evangelism around the world. He presented a structure of prayer that changed everything in my prayer life. His "hour" was composed of twelve five-minute segments with different elements of prayer. I decided to adopt a modified version of his hour and began to structure my prayer time with periods of praise, thanksgiving, confession and repentance, listening, petition, and intercession. This has been an incredibly useful and powerful tool for my prayer life. It gave me a structure of how to pray, and applying it made it absolutely impossible to pray for only a few minutes at a time. Of these elements, praise is by far the cornerstone and most important. I not only meditate on the greatness of God and what he has done but I use Christian music and read a portion of the Psalms or Proverbs as part of my praise time.

A few years after the teaching by Dick Eastman, a second dramatic change took place. This occurred when I listened to a tape by Bill Hybels, the senior pastor at Willow Creek outside Chicago. Surprisingly and with great honesty, Hybels shared his frustration in his prayer life. He shared that the solution for his lack of focus in his prayer time was to write his prayers down. This meant not just keeping a prayer journal but actually writing his prayers down as he was praying. I figured if it was good enough for Bill Hybels, it was certainly good enough for me, and I began to do so. This again changed everything for me. I began to write my prayers down in the composition notebooks that many of us used in college (obviously pre-computer days). These changes made my praying more consistent and much more powerful.

One key in building a consistent and powerful prayer life has been to write down the commitments I have made to pray for people. I keep this part, which is my intercession in prayer, at the back of my prayer journals, where I record what commitments I have made and the wonderful blessings I see when God answers these prayers. Recording intercession this way has enabled me to fulfill the commitments I make to people when I tell them I am going to pray for them. I do not have to remember that I am going to pray because I have written it down. In addition, it has enabled me to follow up with people over the years and share with them that I have been praying for them for days, weeks, months, and in some cases even years. This has surprised and blessed the people I have been praying for and has been a wonderful faith builder for me when I see God answer.

Let me share a couple examples of how God has blessed. Recently I was on the phone with Jennifer (not her real name), an executive assistant to one of the religious leaders of America. I was about to hang up when I asked her if there was anything I could pray for her. First of all she was surprised I would ask, but then she shared that her adult son was facing a very serious addiction problem for which he was currently in prison. She shared he was about to get out and was very concerned about how he would do in the outside world. I prayed with Jennifer on the phone and told her that I would write the prayer request in my Franklin Planner and then transfer it to my prayer journal, which I did. Because I had both the date and the need written down, it was easy for me to call her back in thirty days, sixty days, and then ninety days later to see how she and her son were doing. Jennifer was absolutely flabbergasted that I would remember to pray, would actually do so, and then would take the time to follow up. My response was that if I didn't have time to do that, I was in the wrong ministry and had my priorities upside down. This story is not over yet, and her son continues to face struggles, but I continue to pray along with Jennifer that God will do a mighty work in his life.

Another example of the blessings of praying for others and seeing God work would be the life of Jack Samad, who was a fellow elder with me at two different Presbyterian churches over the years. When Jack was twenty-seven, he was diagnosed with Hodgkin's lymphoma and was given ten years to live. Because of his illness, Jack lived with a sense of urgency in serving Christ, facing the reality that any day might really be his last. While he was still facing his illness, he decided to join the staff of pureHOPE and served the ministry for nearly ten years before God called him home. What a privilege it was for me along with hundreds of others to pray for Jack and to see his life used for the glory of Jesus, not for ten years as the doctors projected but for twenty-eight years. There is no doubt that Jack was sustained by the prayers of God's people, and it was a privilege for me to pray for him. As a dear friend and an incredible partner in ministry, his life was the fruit of the prayers of many, and God blessed.

The last example of prayer life that makes a difference is a very personal one. Recently I was diagnosed with a very rare form of cancer which if untreated is generally fatal within twelve to eighteen months. This came as a great shock to both my wife, Sharon, and me. As my family went through what we called our challenging journey, we were blessed time and time again by the prayers of God's people, including many whom I do not know. I underwent five months of chemotherapy, and God not only sustained me through this period but enabled me to continue to work for pureHOPE and, with only a few exceptions, to feel reasonably good. The thing that really undergirded our lives during this time were the many prayers, notes, phone calls, and emails we received from people who showed the love of Jesus and lifted us to the Lord's throne day after day. During this time, we saw unmistakable signs of the grace of God and his presence.

In my own case in dealing with cancer, the two examples shared above and hundreds of others through the years, I have seen God's blessing through prayer. I do not fully understand how the prayers of the saints intersect with the sovereign power of God, but I believe his promise that he shares with us in James 5 that "the prayers of a righteous man availeth much."

The last significant change in my prayer life took place many years ago, when virtually every day the Lord began to wake me up between 2:00 and 4:00 a.m. When this first started happening, I considered it an interruption in my sleep, but I soon came to believe that this was the Lord's way of getting my attention. So over the years, I have gotten out of bed in the middle of the night, done my quiet time, and by God's grace have been able to go back to sleep very quickly when my prayer time was finished. This has turned out to be a wonderful grace gift to me.

GETTING STARTED

My experience in prayer has been one of the great blessings of my Christian walk. Although I have grown dramatically in spending more time with the Lord and seeing his power and presence, I am still a baby in prayer and have much still to learn. My hope for every believer is that they will grow from where they are today in their prayer lives to become prayer warriors for the kingdom of Christ and for his glory.

Developing structure for my prayers, writing them down, and awakening in the middle of the night to be with God have all proven to help me grow as a man of prayer. There is no question that these tools that have changed me will bless others, but no tool must replace the heart and spirit of prayer: the desire to be with the living God and to spend time with him in quietness.

The Lord has changed me from a frustrated and disappointed disciple in terms of prayer to one whose prayer life is fulfilling, consistent, and powerful. I have seen the Lord answer many prayers over the years. It is a great blessing to me and to those I am praying for. Prayer is one of God's gifts to his people and represents an opportunity to meet with him on a regular basis. Thanks be to him for his wonderful blessings!

BIBLIOGRAPHY

Andy Andrews, *The Butterfly Effect*, Thomas Nelson, 2010

Barry Adams, *The Father's Love Letter*, WingSpread Publisher, 2007

Bill Bright, *The Coming Revival*, Thomas Nelson, Nashville, 1999

Bill Bright, *First Love*, New Life Publications, 2002

Donald Bloesch, *The Struggle of Prayer*, HarperRow, 1980

Jim Cymbala, *The Promises of God's Power*, Zondervan, 2002

Jim Cymbala, *Fresh Wind, Fresh Fire*, Zondervan, 1997

Paul Y. Cho, *Prayer: The Key to Revival*, W Pub Group, 1984

Jonathan Edwards, *The Religious Affections*, Legacy Publications, 2011

Richard Foster, *Celebration of Discipline*, HarperCollins, 1998

Richard Foster, *Prayer, Finding The Heart's True Home*, HarperColins, 1992

Billy Graham, *The Holy Spirit*, Word, 1978

Peter Kreeft, *The God Who Loves You*, Ignatius Press, 1988

Frank Laubauch, *Prayer, the Mightiest Force in the World*, Martino Fine Books, 2012

C. S. Lewis, *Mere Christianity*, HarperCollins, 1944

C. S. Lewis, *Letters to Malcolm Chiefly on Prayer*, Harcourt, 1963

C. S. Lewis, *The Screwtape Letters*, HarperSanFrancisco, 1942

Richard Lovelace, *Dynamics of Spiritual Life*, Downer's Grove, IL, IVP, 1979

Andrew Murray, *With Christ in the School of Prayer*, Merchant Books, 2013

James Bryan Smith, *Embracing the Love of God*, HarperOne, 2008

R. C. Sproul, *The Holiness of God*, Tyndale, 1988

John Stott, *The Message of Ephesians*; God's New Society, IVP 1972

A. W. Tozer, *The Pursuit of God*, HarperRow, 1957

A. W. Tozer, *The Knowledge of the Holy*, HarperRow, 1961

John White, *Daring to Draw Near*, IVP, 1977

AUTHOR BIOGRAPHIES

DR. JERRY KIRK has a Bachelor of Divinity Degree and Master's of Theology Degree from Pittsburgh Theological Seminary and honorary Doctor's Degrees from Grove City College and Sterling College. He was an athlete in both basketball and tennis at the University of Washington playing against UCLA for the PAC conference basketball championship and was captain of the tennis team when they were ranked in the top ten in the nation.

Dr. Kirk pastored three congregations and was Senior Pastor of the College Hill Presbyterian Church for twenty years. During those years, the College Hill Church became an international equipping center for pastors and lay leaders from across the country and many nations in the world through leadership by Dr. Gary Sweeten, Dr. Ron Rand and Mr. Dick and Mrs. Sibyl Towner. He wrote *"The Mind Polluters"* and *"The Homosexual Crisis in the Mainline Church"* published through Word, and wrote the chapter on sexual purity for *"Seven Promises of a Promise Keeper."*

Dr. Kirk founded *pureHOPE* in 1983 and served as chairman of the board until 2009 calling God's people to sexual purity and faithfulness. He founded the *Religious Alliance Against Pornography* in 1986 at the home of Cardinal John J. O'Connor at St. Patrick's Cathedral in New York City. In 2013, through partnership with other leaders, he established *"The Prayer Covenant"* as an organization and ministry to serve as a catalyst for exalting Jesus Christ as Lord and seeking an awakening to the supremacy of Christ.

STEPHEN EYRE: While doing youth ministry and singing in the Christian coffee houses of St. Louis he earned a Masters of Divinity from Covenant Theological Seminary. After 15 years in student ministry with InterVarsity Christian Fellowship he has served churches in Cincinnati as *Pastor of Discipleship, Executive Pastor,* and *Minister of Congregational Development.* He is also the *Director of the C. S. Lewis Institute of Cincinnati* that provides a course of discipleship in the thoughtful tradition of C. S. Lewis and seeks to cultivate both mind and heart.

His first book, *Defeating the Dragons of the World* explored ways in which the American church is infected and compromised by a secularizing culture. His book *Drawing Close to God,* reframes the traditional "quiet time" incorporating spiritual practices and disciplines in ways that are accessible and practical. He has published twelve Bible study discussion guides (IVP, Victor, Zondervan) and a series of eight *Spiritual Encounter Guides,* (IVP) as resources for guided quiet times.